The Movement in Acts

Encouraging the Saints Toward a Movement

Dr. Oscar T. Moses

sermonto**book**
.com

Sincere appreciation, love, and respect are given to the love of my life, my wife, the brilliant Dr. Jacqueline Marie Moses, for providing loving support, honest feedback, and ongoing encouragement. The writer is lovingly and eternally grateful to his loving parents, Rosetta Moses Hill and the late Oscar Moses, for providing a model of discipleship and a Christian home. The writer expresses great love and appreciation to his only sibling, David A. Moses, his wife Kelly, and their two children, Taylor V. Moses and David Andrew Moses, for providing ongoing loving support.

Special appreciation to a few mentors in ministry: Rev. William R. Lott, Dr. Joel D. Taylor, Dr. Richard Nelson, Rev. Frank McSwain, Rev. Stephen J. Thurston, and Rev. Jimmy Burnside for their spiritual guidance and prayerful support.

Special appreciation and gratitude goes to the entire membership of The Mount Hermon Missionary Baptist church for their patience and willingness to participate in the process to develop this model of ministry.

Finally, above all, praise to God for His sovereign existence, love, promises, providence, and challenge to the church.

CONTENTS

Note from the Author 3

Jesus Is Ready 5

The Birth of a Movement 9

The Committed Church 21

God's Power Presented 35

The Power Resisted 43

Protecting the Integrity of the Church 55

The Source of All Strength 67

Production Through Persecution 79

Facilitating the Spread of the Gospel 87

Changing Perspectives 99

Penetrating Prejudices 109

Changing Attitudes 117

The Power of a Praying Church 125

Equipping Those God Calls 133

Power, Perseverance, Partnership, and Prudence 143

Setting Standards for the Saints 151

The Holy Navigator 163

The Holy Spirit Reasons 169

Affirmation, Assurance, and Assistance 175

Victorious over the Occult 181

Empowering the Saints to Completion 189

The Sustainer of Ministry 195

The Power of Personal Testimonies 201

Courage to Stay the Course 209

A Christian Character and a Clear Conscience 215

The Provider of Patience 221

Creating Consistent Lives...229

Confidence for Life's Dark Storms 233

A Consistent Conclusion 239

In the Center of His Will—and Unstoppable 245

Notes..247

About the Author...256

About Sermon To Book..259

Note from the Author

The Movement in Acts is essentially an extended study guide for the book of Acts. It was designed and written to enlighten, empower, and engage congregations in the work of evangelism through the power of the Holy Spirit.

My intent is to express that God never intended the "Movement" in the early church to cease. The problem that has emerged within the twenty-first-century church is a failure to comprehend that the church is not just an institution but also a movement. The modern church has abandoned the power given her in the first century.

Each chapter of this book describes how the power of the Holy Spirit used ordinary people to effect God's plan of salvation victoriously against great opposition.

The supplementary workbook for *The Movement in Acts* summarizes each chapter of the book with review questions designed to engage church members and other readers in the Bible study process. Some chapters also offer "Group Questions" intended for group study and individual critical reflection. Each workbook section concludes with an application-oriented action step and a notes page for you to jot down important information, thoughts, and questions as you read.

Whatever your purposes in reading *The Movement in Acts*, let it inspire you and all the saints to sustain and grow the Spirit-led movement of Christ in the church—and in the world!

—*Dr. Oscar T. Moses*

INTRODUCTION

Jesus Is Ready

The church of Jesus Christ was intended to be far more than an institution but a movement. Jesus said in Matthew 16:18, "Upon this rock I will build my church; and the gates of hell shall not prevail against it" (KJV). Gates are designed to keep some people out and to keep others in. Gates do not move. Gates are defensive. The church of Jesus Christ should be concerned for those who are being kept behind the gates of hell—knowing Satan will do everything to keep them trapped in.

In Matthew 16:18, Jesus clearly stated the church was to be offensively on the move prevailing over the gates of hell and rescuing lost souls who are being held hostage by Satan. Though Jesus said the church would be victorious over the gates of hell, it appears as though the gates of hell are overcoming the church.

People are abandoning the church in large numbers. Churches are closing all over the country. If the church is supposed to triumph over the gates, as Jesus said, what seems to be the problem?

The problem is the church has abandoned the power Jesus promised her. Jurgen Moltmann wrote in his book *Religion, Revolution and the Future*, "Many are abandoning Christianity because they can find in it no power of the future."[1] In today's culture, most people believe churches have no power to change the "hellish" conditions of people's lives. This problem has emerged because the church has failed to understand it is not just an institution but also a movement. Church is more than a clique or a country club; it is a place where people become empowered to carry out the movement that Jesus set in motion more than two thousand years ago.

The church lacks power because she has abandoned the power given to her to become victorious over the gates of hell. Consequently, the church is no longer a movement of the Savior, but a museum for saints where people assemble to stare without departing to serve. The church is often the gathering place for many, Sunday after Sunday, where lives are not changed, people are not saved, and the gates of hell are alive and doing well. Yet, in the book of Acts we see the first church operating much differently. The early church movement reveals a church that operated in the power of the Holy Spirit and made a difference in the lives of people. The question for the modern church is how do we get back to the movement of God?

Context of Acts

The Book of Acts is the second chapter of a continued story that began in the book of Luke, a volume that Luke sent to Theophilus. Luke wrote Acts to give a detailed history of the church. In his gospel, Luke told the story of the life of Jesus upon earth. In Acts, he tells the story of the Christian church and the overwhelming power that launched a movement.

In Acts, the reader will discover that the whole lesson of Acts is, as William Barclay wrote, "Jesus is not a 'just was' but He still lives and the life of the church goes on through Him."[2] In other words, Christ is the power that propelled the movement of the early church—and He is ready to do so in the church today!

CHAPTER ONE

The Birth of a Movement

Acts 1

It is not for you to know the times or the seasons, which the Father hath put in his own power. But ye shall receive power, after that the Holy Ghost is come upon you: and ye shall be witnesses unto me both in Jerusalem, and in all Judea and in Samaria, and unto the uttermost parts of the earth. — Acts 1:7–8 (KJV)

Something new happened at Calvary. A motley band of men who had followed one Jewish rabbi for three years were forever changed. As they witnessed their teacher suffer and die on the cross, resurrect three days later, and then ascend to heaven, they were enabled to do something profound—to impact a dark and hopeless world and reflect the light of the very presence of God. It was the beginning of a movement God never intended would end, a movement that would take a level of commitment beyond their capability.

Power to Witness

The scene in Acts 1:7–8 took place on the Mount of Olives just before Jesus uttered His last words before departing earth. However, the problem at hand was with Jesus' disciples, whom He was about to leave in charge of His church. These eleven men were concerned about their lack of power and discernment. Because the Jewish people had suffered so much under Roman domination, they wanted to know when Jesus would make Israel an independent nation. They were preoccupied with matters that should not have been a priority. They wanted power, but the *wrong* kind of power— they wanted political power to dominate their oppressor.

Let's look at Acts 1:8 closer. Jesus said His followers would receive power from the Holy Ghost. This was not political power or financial power, or even power to dominate their enemies. Rather, the power His disciples would receive would enable them to witness about Him all over the world. This was not a command but a statement of fact. When the Holy Ghost comes upon a person, He provides the ability to talk about Jesus. The phrase "shall be," in the phrase "Ye shall be witnesses unto me..." (Acts 1:8 KJV), is in the indicative mood as opposed to the imperative. This indicates Jesus' words were not a suggestion but a statement that meant "this will be."

A witness is a person who says, "I know this is true." A witness does not say, "I think or presume," but "I know!" In the original Greek, the word for witness is *martys*, where the English word 'martyr' comes from.[3]

A 'martyr' is someone willing to sacrifice his or her life as a witness to a cause. Therefore, a person is made a witness not only by what he says but also by what he does. Their life should reflect their witness. How believers live their life should be a reflection of the character of Christ—a witness to Him.

Jesus said the disciples would witness "in Jerusalem, and in all Judaea, and in Samaria, and unto the uttermost part of the earth" (Acts 1:8 KJV). Jerusalem was the *familiar* place where Jesus was killed by the mob. Judea was the *resistant* place that challenged Jesus' ministry. Samaria was the *rejected* place where known religious "half-breeds" and outcasts lived. The uttermost parts of the earth were the *foreign* places where people knew nothing about Jesus.

These four places represent places of evangelism in the believer's life. Jerusalem represents people close to you and close to where you live. You don't have to be a missionary in Africa to witness for Christ! The best place to be a witness is in your home and in your neighborhood with the people you already know. Rather than flying through the grocery store without making eye contact or talking with anyone, work to build relationships with the checkers and the baggers. Take the time to talk to the older man or woman who lives down the street, who may not be able to attend church. Spend time with your mother-in-law, trusting God for the power to do so. Your life will become a witness to Christ while you go about daily activities.

Judea and Samaria represent cross-cultural boundaries. Judea was a Roman province and Samaria was a place where so-called "half-breeds" (foreigners who intermarried with Israelites) and those who were cast out of society lived. The Jews and Samaritans had been at odds for hundreds of years. Recall John 4 and the story of the Samaritan woman at the well. The first thing the woman said was, "Jews have no dealings with the Samaritans" (John 4:9 KJV). Jesus was teaching His disciples, and thus Christians today, the importance of setting aside racial differences for the sake of the gospel. Dr. Martin Luther King Jr. used the power of words and acts of non-violent resistance—such as protests, grassroots organizing, and civil disobedience—to show that regardless of color or creed, all people are equal members of the human family. His life was a witness to Christ.[4]

Finally, Jesus commanded His disciples to go to "the uttermost part of the earth" (Acts 1:8 KJV). This meant to take this gospel to the four corners of the earth, or to different cultures and lands. Hundreds of years before Jesus made this statement in Acts 1:8, the psalmist wrote, "Ask of me, and I shall give thee the heathen for thine inheritance, and the uttermost parts of the earth for thy possession" (Psalm 2:8 KJV). God always intended for the gospel to go out to the whole world!

Until He Returns...

After the disciples watched Jesus ascend into heaven, they remained standing and looking up into the sky. Suddenly, two men appeared dressed in white robes. They said, "Ye men of Galilee, why stand ye gazing up into heaven? this same Jesus, which is taken up from you into heaven, shall so come in like manner as ye have seen him go into heaven" (Acts 1:11 KJV). Within twenty-four hours after Jesus ascended to heaven leaving this promise, the disciples receive three thousand brand new believers in the church. The church movement had begun.

However, it was never supposed to end. Near the end of His life, Jesus' disciples had asked Him what signs would alert them to His return (Matthew 24:3). Matthew 24:14 says, "And this gospel of the kingdom will be preached in the whole world as a testimony to all nations, and then the end will come" (NIV). Jesus' own words indicate the church movement should have never ceased. His mandate in Matthew 24:24, and throughout the Scriptures, was to carry the gospel message out until the end when He returned.

By 2017, the church movement had slowed down to almost a trickle. The Holy Ghost has sponsored the movement, and the church must realize that it has abandoned the power to evangelize as Jesus promised us in Acts 1:8. Here it is! What use is power if it is not used?

Change Precedes a New Movement

Whenever a movement begins, it is usually because there is a need for change.

One such push for change that resulted in a movement occurred on December 1, 1955. Rosa Parks was arrested in Montgomery, Alabama, for refusing to give up her seat on a city bus to a white man. Word spread throughout the African American community and the community had enough. After several phone calls, a group of African American women decided to call for a boycott of the city buses. Black preachers and leaders joined the movement.

Four days later, a rally was held at the Holt Street Baptist Church in Montgomery, and the women decided to carry out the boycott. They were inspired by the words of the Reverend Dr. Martin Luther King Jr., who had made a case for peace and nonviolence. He declared the movement would not mirror the Ku Klux Klan's work, but would be guided by higher standards of Christian faith. Love must be the regulating ideal. A movement was birthed out of a need for change!

Similarly, Jesus initiated a new movement, but change was necessary for that movement to be birthed and grow: a change in humanity's posture toward Him. Rather than people continuing to unsuccessfully achieve a relationship with God through personal effort, Jesus preached salvation through grace by faith in Him. Everyone who believed in Him "should not perish, but have eternal life" (John 3:15 KJV).

As a result of this change in people's hearts, the church movement began.

Birthing a Movement

Fuller Theological Seminary professor Dr. Bobby Clinton has studied movements for many years. He says that a movement is a "groundswell of people that are committed."[5] This is what happened in the early church. People were committed to the Master's mandate and they convinced others to join. The critical question is: How does the modern church birth a movement? There are four things the church must commit to that will keep the church movement alive.

A Commitment to Revisit the Scriptures

Sometimes it's necessary to go backwards to go forward. This is what the Africans call a *Sankofa* experience—a return to go back and get it.[6] The Bible gives instruction on how God intended for the church to grow, and yet for some reason the Scriptures have been cast aside. Human ideas, a business mindset, and a secular, corporate ideology have replaced the Word of God. Churches must return to the Scriptures and the instruction God has left for believers in order for God's church movement to continue.

A Commitment to Revealing a New Reality

When people realize what they can receive from change is better than what they have, excitement begins to brew. This is true of the gospel, as well. The tragedy and threat to any movement is when those who are supposed to be a part of it can't see the good in change. For an effective movement there must be hope in what could be, the commitment to press on towards a new mark, and defiant resistance to defeat. For effective church evangelism, churches must commit to fix their eyes on Jesus, "the author and finisher of our faith; who for the joy that was set before him endured the cross, despising the shame, and is set down at the right hand of the throne of God" (Hebrews 12:2 KJV). Believers must press on toward this goal, and resist opposition.

A Commitment to Release Power

Paul wrote to his young disciple Timothy that God has not given followers of Jesus a spirit of fear, "but of power, and of love, and of a sound mind" (2 Timothy 1:7 KJV). Every Christian has the power of God within them, but collectively God's people have become timid in releasing its power. The church displays God's power when its people come together, united in vision, purpose, and action. When God's people are divided, the manifestation of His power is diminished.

A Commitment to Remember the End Game

The end game will occur when Jesus returns for the committed church. Don't stand around staring, but get busy because Jesus is coming back again. God has gifted His children with many things for the purpose of growing His Kingdom. Illustrating this concept, Jesus taught His followers the parable of the talents—where He challenged His hearers to faithfully steward the life God has given (Matthew 25:14–30). Though the parable is speaking about money and what different men did with the talents given to them, the deeper meaning has to do the condition of a person's heart.

Repentance is mentioned seventy times in the Bible. Baptism is mentioned twenty times, and the new birth is mentioned nine times. But Jesus promised 318 times in the New Testament alone that He is coming to this earth again. Remember the end game and press on in obedience for the Kingdom until Jesus returns!

There are many speculations about the return of Christ but the truth is, "no one knows, not even the angels in heaven, nor the Son, but only the Father" (Matthew 24:36 NIV). This same Jesus who was born of a virgin named Mary, baptized by John the Baptist, and tempted by the devil after a forty day fast is returning. Jesus, who turned water to wine at Cana, raised Lazarus from the dead, was betrayed and sold by Judas, and forsaken by His disciples, who was denied by Peter, and condemned even though innocent by the Sanhedrin, is returning. Jesus, who was crucified horribly by Pilate, was buried by His disciples, and arose triumphant from the dead by the power of the Holy Ghost...this *same* Jesus is coming back. This truth should cause believers to rejoice in what is ahead, and unite as a church to continue the movement that began when Jesus came to earth the first time.

Play On

Let's circle back to the concept of a witness. A witness, or martyr is someone willing to sacrifice his or her life. It is one who is willing to die for a cause. The birth of a movement begins with people who are committed to go down with the ship.

During the taping of the *The Kings of Comedy*, Steve Harvey told a joke about the Titanic's last hours. As the ship was sinking, a group of eight men employed to offer music during the cruise—who had played throughout the entire voyage—continued to play when their death was imminent. Mr. Harvey found it impossible to believe how those musicians could gather, sit, and play music together while the ship was going down. A freelance journalist and author named Steve Turner even wrote a book about this called *The Band That Played On*.[7]

In his book, Turner revealed the truth behind the question of why the band played on. The leader of the group of eight musicians was a violinist by the name of Wallace Hartley from a small town in Lancashire, England, who was a Christian. Hartley was personable, cheerful, and always attended church when he was back on land. Hartley made two comments that reveal why he decided, as the band's leader, to keep playing. During an interview with a British newspaper, he had been asked what he would do if he were ever on a sinking ship. Hartley had replied, "I don't think I would do better than play 'Oh God Our Help in Ages Past' or 'Nearer, My God, to Thee.'" Those were the final songs played while the Titanic succumbed to the ocean.

What better way for those thousands of passengers to depart this world and open their eyes on the other side to see Christ, than to hear playing, as they took their last breath, "Oh God Our Help in Ages Past" or "Nearer, My God, to Thee." As my friend Pastor Richard Wilford has observed, "Why cut and run, when you can stay and play?"

Followers of Jesus have a profound opportunity to direct people to God like the band on the Titanic. But they must be committed to sacrifice their wants, needs, and desires for others. They must be willing to testify to Christ, even if it means going down with the ship.

Calvary was the birth of a movement of people committed to giving their life to be witnesses for Christ. Jesus could have cut and run but instead He stayed and played. He could have called ten thousand angels to relieve Him of His duties, but He knew that His blood shed would spark a movement. He was so committed to the movement that He was willing to die. His dying brought pain to the movement but His resurrection brought power!

Because He lives, believers can face tomorrow. Because He lives, all fear is gone. Because He lives, the movement shall never end!

CHAPTER TWO

The Committed Church

Acts 2

*And they continued steadfastly in the apostles' doctrine and
fellowship, and in breaking of bread, and in prayers.*
— *Acts 2:42 (KJV)*

God is looking for committed Christians. The late
E.M. Bounds said, "The church is looking for better
methods; God is looking for better men and women."[8]
Another quote on commitment from an unknown author
states: "Commitment means staying loyal to what you
said you were going to do long after the mood you said it
in has left you."

Unfortunately, many churches lack committed people.
A lack of commitment leads to despondency and sub-par
results. This is not how God intended the church to
continue. It may seem like there is no need to commit to
church, but committing to serving God results in

unexpected changes. Help often becomes available from unforeseen, unimaginable sources. Commitment invokes the power of God in people's lives.

Levels of Commitment

There are three ways people prioritize church. Some people approach church casually. These half-hearted churchgoers make involvement with the church an option and not a priority. Church is what they do when they have nothing else to do.

Others approach church critically. These hard-hearted folks find an issue with what everyone else is doing wrong. Their joy is contingent upon others' commitment to the church and not theirs. In most instances, the critique does not match the level of commitment.

A third group approaches church consistently. These hopeful-hearted people understand that when they take care of God's business He takes care of theirs, and the only thing that will carry over from this life is what they do out of love for God. They know there is good news available when people commit themselves to the Lord.

God moves in the lives of committed people. But, how do we get the power of God to move in our lives?

The Bible reveals the first church operated in a unique and profound way—one that centered on unabashed commitment to the One its people followed.

The First Church

In Acts 1, Jesus had instructed the disciples to remain in Jerusalem until the promise of the Father arrived. Acts 2 reveals the fulfillment of the promise—the coming of the Spirit—and the response of the church.

The chapter begins with the disciples all together in one place on the Feast of Pentecost (Acts 2:1). 'Pentecost' is the Greek adjective *pentēkostē* meaning, "the fiftieth day."[9] As the name suggests, Pentecost occurred fifty days after the Passover celebration. According to the law of Moses, this feast was celebrated by offering the first fruits of the wheat harvest.

Acts 2 provides a detailed account of the historic birth of the church in Jerusalem in what Paul described as an upper room (Acts 1:13). From out of nowhere, without warning, a strong wind filled the building.

It was the Holy Spirit. Paul described this event in detail in Acts 2:3-4: "And there appeared unto them cloven tongues like as of fire, and it sat upon each of them. And they were all filled with the Holy Ghost, and began to speak with other tongues, as the Spirit gave them utterance" (KJV). The disciples began to speak other languages that they had never spoken before. Many foreigners staying in Jerusalem recognized the disciples were speaking in their own native tongue and were amazed (Acts 2:6). Some thought the disciples were drunk off of cheap wine (Acts 2:13).

However, Peter arose and declared what had really occurred is now known as the very first sermon. The other eleven apostles supported him. Peter spoke with urgency and passion explaining that they were not drunk at such an early hour rather described the event as prophetic. He reminded his audience of the prophet Joel and said:

> And it shall come to pass in the last days, saith God, I will pour out of my Spirit upon all flesh: and your sons and your daughters shall prophesy, and your young men shall see visions, and your old men shall dream dreams: And on my servants and on my handmaidens I will pour out in those days of my Spirit; and they shall prophesy: And I will shew wonders in heaven above, and signs in the earth beneath; blood, and fire, and vapour of smoke: The sun shall be turned into darkness, and the moon into blood, before that great and notable day of the Lord come: And it shall come to pass, that whosoever shall call on the name of the Lord shall be saved. – *Acts 2:17–21 (KJV)*

After Peter's sermon, the Bible says those who were listening were "pricked in their heart" (Acts 2:37 KJV) and wanted to know what they should do next. Peter appealed to those who were present and said, "Repent, and be baptized every one of you in the name of Jesus Christ for the remission of sins, and ye shall receive the gift of the Holy Ghost. For the promise is unto you, and to your children, and to all that are afar off, even as many as the LORD our God shall call" (Acts 2:38-39 KJV). Peter appealed for their salvation; that day, three thousand people put their faith in Jesus, and the first church was birthed.

Steadfast Practices

Acts 2:42 says,

And they continued steadfastly in the apostles' doctrine and fellowship, and in breaking of bread, and in prayers. (KJV)

This particular verse speaks to the early church members' level of commitment which laid the foundation for its success. They continued to do something that blessed both the church and their very lives. The early Christians continued steadfastly. The word 'steadfastly' is the Greek word *proskartereō*. *Proskartereō* is a compound word made up of the preposition *pros*, which means "to, toward or in the direction of," followed by *kartereō*, a verb with the root concept of "to be strong or firm." Thus, *proskartereō* literally means "to be strong toward something or someone.[10] The phrase "continued steadfastly" means the disciples never stopped studying the apostles' doctrine, breaking bread together, and praying. These activities were a common practice and way of life

In the New Testament, this phrase "continued steadfastly" carries the meaning of being committed. Acts 2:42 teaches the early church members were strongly devoted to some practices that were never meant to cease.

Loyal Devotion

This idea of loyal commitment to the church was reflected in four ways according to Paul: in the apostles' doctrine, in their fellowship, in the collective breaking of bread, and in prayer.

The Truth: The Apostles' Doctrine

Preachers have the profound responsibility of expounding God's Word truthfully. Those who were saved in Acts 2 trusted in the preacher's words. They were committed to knowing who Jesus was and what He had done in the lives of His followers. They were committed to the Word.

In modern times, once a preacher *proclaims* something the follower of Christ has the unique ability to investigate it personally. However, this is often lacking; often the only time people hear or read Scripture is on Sunday. People within the church must be committed to the Word of God, "the apostle's doctrine."

The Tie: Fellowship

The word 'fellowship' comes from the Greek word *koinōnia*, meaning "association, community, communion, joint participation or intercourse," and also, "intimacy."[11] It carries the idea of sharing in something with another. There must be some fellowship among the believers—intimacy in relationship—if they are to impact on the world. Jesus said that "all men know that ye are my disciples, if ye have love one to another" (John 13:35 KJV). If Jesus' church does not love one another, the world notices.

Christians must learn to love one another. Paul said early church members were continually committed to fellowship with one another. When people in the church have no connection with one another, they are prone to go in different directions.

The Table: The Breaking of Bread

The Syriac (the Aramaic interpretation of the Scriptures) defines this statement of "the breaking of bread" as the "eucharist," or the Lord's Supper.[12] This meant they were committed to remembering the sacrifice that Jesus made on Calvary. First Corinthians 11:26 says, "For as often as ye eat this bread, and drink this cup, ye do shew the Lord's death till he come" (KJV). The church must be committed to continually remembering what Jesus Christ did on the cross through the celebration of communion—through the act of breaking bread.

The Throne: Prayer

The church must also be committed to prayer. When the church prays, things happen—especially when the church prays "with one accord" (Acts 1:14 KJV). Collective prayer is powerful; people are delivered, sick people are healed, and mean people become sweet.

Prayer changes people even if it does not change their situation.

When the church operates in this way, continually believing God's Word, fellowshipping and breaking break together, and praying as a corporate body, the power of God is manifested.

Modern-Day Movements

When the power of God comes alive in a church, a movement starts and movements start when people are committed. Ponder the movements that have taken place in the world. Not all are godly; nonetheless, people were committed to them.

One example would be the LGBT movement. The last decade has yielded tremendous success for this once-marginal movement, which is active worldwide.

Another example is the 2009 Tea Party movement, which began to flourish after President Obama's first inauguration when his administration announced plans to give financial aid to bankrupt homeowners. Tea Partiers are known for their conservative positions and their support of the Republican Party. The Tea Party movement gained momentum as its members vehemently opposed every policy President Obama tried to implement, particularly universal healthcare. Various polls have found that slightly over 10 percent of Americans identify as members.[13]

A third movement, The Black Lives Matter (BLM) movement, surfaced in 2014 when George Zimmerman was aquitted in the shooting death of African American teen Trayvon Martin. It emerged as a movement that campaigned against violence towards black people, particularly brutality from the police. The movement received momentum after the deaths of African Americans Michael Brown and Eric Garner.

Movements are sustained by a passionate commitment for a common interest to be heard. The church movement should be fueled by a passion commitment for the gospel to go out!

A Powerless Church?

The movement of the church seems to have come to a screeching halt. Because of this, its people must ask the critical questions: "Are we a part of a movement? Or are we in maintenance mode to keep the church relevant?"

One question many Christians cannot answer correctly is: "Now that you are a member of the church what does God expect of you?" Well, the answer is not difficult at all. God expects for His people to continue the movement that began with the early church—to wholeheartedly commit to be a witness for Christ to the world.

God never intended for Christians or the church to be powerless. Jesus promised believers would receive His power upon belief in Christ (Acts 1:8). The Bible also says God has not given His people the spirit of fear but of power, love, and a sound mind (2 Timothy 2:1–7). Paul said in Ephesians 3:21 that Jesus will receive the glory out of the power that works in believers.

Yet Christians do not seem to be operating in this power—and if the church ever needed God's power it is now, and it is available for all believers.

There are four levels of commitment that will help you to experience His power in ways never experienced before.

Commitment to Sharing Jesus

Every Christian should be an evangelist. Begin talking about the goodness of Jesus Christ in your life instead of everything you find wrong. Evangelism is merely sharing the transforming power of Jesus Christ with others. Develop a "Forrest Gump" mentality—if someone sits next to you they have to hear your story of how your live has changed since believing in Jesus. Tell the world God transformed you!

Commitment to Serving in a Ministry

God has gifted every person who trusts Him to do something for the purpose of ministry—serving for the purpose of bringing glory to God. He leaves no one out. All hands are needed on deck of the ship if it is going to float. Get busy serving God and He will pour out His power to serve Him more. Don't ask Him for power and then refuse to use it to meet the needs of others. Serve in a ministry—even if it is in a small capacity. God will reveal where the gifts He has given are manifested most powerfully!

Commitment to Studying God's Word

Finally, commit to learning more about God and knowing Him more intimately this year than ever. Challenge yourself to increase Bible study, and perhaps begin memorizing larger portions of Scripture. This is how the believer comes to know God; there will be no excuse for not knowing Him when you stand before the Lord.

Commitment to Sunday Mornings

Don't commit to coming three Sundays out of a month to church, but come every Sunday. You never know when you will get your breakthrough. Commitment is needed for the long haul. The writer of Hebrews said, "Wherefore seeing we are compassed about with so great a cloud of witnesses … let us run with patience the race that is set before us" (Hebrews 12:1 KJV). Get back in the race, even when exhaustion, or hurt, or betrayal comes. Run and don't turn back.

Brothers and sisters, life is a not a sprint but a marathon. Commitment means no turning back but giving the best you have.

In 1519 Spanish conquistador Hernando Cortez arrived off the coast of what is now knows as Mexico with ships, a few horses, and about six hundred soldiers. He was on a mission to capture the Aztec treasure and impose Spanish rule. Fearing that his soldiers would not be fully committed to the battle, Cortez gave the order to "burn the boats," eliminating the possibility of retreat, and forcing his men to fight and win.

In the same way, believers need to ask the Lord to "burn some boats" in their life to lead them to commitment. Examine areas in your life that may be pulling you away from being fully committed to the battle—habits, addictions, or even people. Decide if it's time to remove those things from your life in order to be fully available to God for the mission of expanding His Kingdom.

I thank God for His church. Modern thought is the church serves no purpose. That sounds philosophical and has a bit of new age movement nuance to it. But those who have been born again understand God's people are the apple of His eye (Zechariah 2:8). Those who have been born again recognize the level of commitment God has for the church. He displayed His level of commitment through His Son Jesus. Romans 5:8 says, "But God commendeth his love toward us, in that, while we were yet sinners, Christ died for us" (KJV). Jesus Christ came to the world to die for mankind's sins. He committed Himself to the charge. Jesus, fully human while being fully divine, likely felt like giving up but He didn't turn back. He set His sights on Calvary to give the best that He could give the world. He could have come down off of the cross but He stayed there, even referencing this idea of commitment while dying. Crying out to His Father Jesus said, "Into thy hands I commend my Spirit" (Luke 23:46 KJV). Commitment is a life entrusted to God, modeled perfectly by Jesus at the cross.

Commitment means your heart is fixed and your mind is made up. In my mind I hear the late Pat Stewart singing:

> Heaven is my goal each and every day. I've got to keep on moving in the right way. If I stumble along the way step aside don't you block my way. I don't want anybody stumbling over me.[14]

There is a beautiful old hymn by an anonymous author which communicates this level of commitment in its chorus: "I have decided to follow Jesus, no turning back, no turning back."[15]

Can you say the same?

CHAPTER THREE

God's Power Presented

Acts 3

And as the lame man which was healed held Peter and John, all the people ran together unto them in the porch that is called Solomon's, greatly wondering. And when Peter saw it, he answered unto the people, Ye men of Israel, why marvel ye at this? or why look ye so earnestly on us, as though by our own power or holiness we had made this man to walk? — Acts 3:11–12 (KJV)

When God's people trust Him and respond to Him with commitment to be a witness, His power is released. The impact often goes beyond what the child of God can begin to comprehend. Many times, the believer will never know just how far reaching one act of obedience will go—like the ripple effect produced when a stone is dropped into water.

In Acts 3, Peter and John, unified in Spirit, stepped out into their Jerusalem to make known God's power to others through the good news of Jesus Christ. It is a lesson for believers today of the power of God available to those who believe! (Romans 1:16).

The Power of the Gospel

In Acts 3, Peter and John ascended to the temple courts at the hour of prayer where they encountered a lame beggar who was begging at the temple gate. The beggar asked the two disciples for money, and according to the Scriptures, Peter and John were required by God's law to help such people. They knew the Scriptures that said, "Thou shalt not harden thine heart, nor shut thine hand from thy poor brother: But thou shalt open thine hand wide unto him, and shalt surely lend him sufficient for his need" (Deuteronomy 15:7–8 KJV). It was not uncommon, therefore, for beggars to ask for money in Jesus' day.

However, Peter responded, "Silver and gold have I none; but such as I have give I thee: In the name of Jesus Christ of Nazareth rise up and walk" (Acts 3:6 KJV). The beggar's feet inexplicably became strong, and he jumped up. He could walk! More importantly, he *believed.*

Peter offered the beggar so much more than a few coins to pay for another meal; He offered him eternal life in Jesus Christ—healing the man both physically and spiritually as He presented the power of Jesus to him. This is what God is calling believers to do: to present the power of Jesus to a watching world.

The World Is Watching!

Scripture says that as Peter pulled the beggar up, he began "walking, and leaping, and praising God" (Acts 3:8 KJV). Two verses later, in Acts 3:10, the Bible says onlookers were amazed and filled with awe.

There was an audience that day at the temple gate, and Peter and John didn't miss the opportunity in front of them. They proceeded to preach to anyone who would listen about Jesus Christ crucified, buried and resurrected from the dead. Peter admonished the crowd for the people's surprise of this miracle and assured them that what they had witnessed was not of their own power, but God's promise fulfilled through the Holy Ghost. The God of Abraham, Isaac, and Jacob had glorified His Son Jesus Christ.

Within the context of Peter's sermon, he reminded his listeners of how they rejected Jesus Christ and asked for a murderer to be set free before Pilate. Jesus was indeed crucified at the people's request, but God raised Him from the dead and He lives. Peter's sermon informed the crowd that Jesus, whom they killed, was alive. It was through the lame man's faith in a resurrected Jesus that he was healed.

Peter followed this miracle with a history lesson within the context of his sermon; their hearts were open, sensitive because of the miracle they had just witnessed. He reminded the onlookers what God said through the preaching of His prophets; God's Messiah would come and suffer: "shewed by the mouth of all his prophets, that Christ should suffer, he hath so fulfilled" (Acts 3:18

KJV). God knew from the beginning of time His people would betray Jesus the Messiah but He would use that event to fulfill His plans for the redemption of the world.

Peter directed the listeners to repent and change their way so that God could wipe away their sins and shower His blessings upon them:

Repent ye therefore, and be converted, that your sins may be blotted out, when the times of refreshing shall come from the presence of the Lord.

> *And he shall send Jesus Christ, which before was preached unto you: Whom the heaven must receive until the times of restitution of all things, which God hath spoken by the mouth of all his holy prophets since the world began.* — *Acts 3:20–21 (KJV)*

Peter concluded his sermon by informing the hearer what would happen if they rejected the Word of God from the mouths of his prophets from Moses all the way down the prophetic line you will be lost:

> *Ye are the children of the prophets, and of the covenant which God made with our fathers, saying unto Abraham, And in thy seed shall all the kindreds of the earth be blessed. Unto you first God, having raised up his Son Jesus, sent him to bless you, in turning away every one of you from his iniquities.* — *Acts 3:25–26 (KJV)*

Peter commanded believers to present God's power to a watching world. His Holy Spirit took over from there. This same power that brought Jesus back from the dead is available to others. Committed members of the church of Jesus Christ will long to help others see the power of God.

The Function of the Holy Spirit

But what—or who—is the Holy Spirit? How and why does the Spirit move with the power of God in our lives, and how are we to respond?

The role that the Holy Spirit plays within the individual believer's life, and within the life of the church, is not often discussed in modern-day churches. However, it is important for every believer to understand the power and presence of the Holy Spirit as it relates to their life and to the body.

The Holy Spirit is a being, and as such it is appropriate to use the pronouns 'He' or 'Him' when referencing Him. The Holy Spirit is the third person of the Godhead: God the Father, God the Son, and God the Holy Spirit.

Jesus came to earth to complete a mighty work and He finished it. He came to live and die as a sacrifice for the sins of the world, and He did. When the earthly work of Jesus ended the followers of Jesus' work began and this work has yet to be completed. The believer's work is carried by the Holy Spirit for the purpose of bringing the lost to salvation.

The Holy Spirit performs a number of functions to enable the ambassador of Christ to be able to carry out His commission to bring the gospel of salvation to a lost world.

The Holy Spirit Seals Believers Forever

In Ephesians Paul 1:13 said, "In whom ye also trusted, after that ye heard the word of truth, the gospel of your salvation: in whom also after that ye believed, ye were sealed with that holy Spirit of promise" (KJV), and in Ephesians 4:30 he said, "And grieve not the holy Spirit of God, whereby ye are sealed unto the day of redemption" (KJV). In both verses Paul indicated the Holy Spirit seals believers forever. This means that once a person is saved the Holy Spirit seals that salvation and it cannot be reversed or tampered with. This sealing happens the moment a person accepts Christ, and it is a one-time event.

The Holy Spirit Fills Frequently and Feels Fervently

Although the believer is sealed with the Holy Spirit only one time, they are *filled* with the Spirit on a continuous basis. Paul said in Ephesians 5:18 that believers are "not drunk with wine, wherein is excess; but be filled with the Spirit" (KJV). This phrase "filled with the Spirit," where 'spirit' is with a capital S, shows up in Scripture only once, here in Ephesians 5:18. Peter wanted his hearers to know the filling of the Spirit is not a one-time event but a moment-by-moment choice each believer must commit to.

Ephesians 5:18 sets the tone for the repeat filling of the Holy Spirit. The word for 'fill' is the Greek word *plēroō*. *Plēroō* is equivalent to a flood that overflows. It means "to make full, to fill up, or to fill to the full," like a pouring a cup of water to the point where it's about to overflow over the cup's rim.[16]

All people, even followers of Christ, will experience low seasons in life. It is during those times the Holy Spirit is ready to repeatedly fill the believer. When the follower of Jesus can't take another step forward, the power of the Spirit will enable him to press on.

The Holy Spirit also *feels* believers when they are low. The writer of Hebrews 4:15 declared that unlike Old Testament priests Jesus is a greater priest who can feel His people's sin: "For we have not an high priest which cannot be touched with the feeling of our infirmities; but was in all points tempted like as we are, yet without sin" (Hebrews 4:15 KJV). The apostle John described the Holy Spirit as the Comforter that Christ sent for when His people are low:

> But the Comforter, which is the Holy Ghost, whom the Father will send in my name, he shall teach you all things, and bring all things to your remembrance, whatsoever I have said unto you. — *John 14:26 (KJV)*

The Holy Spirit both fills and feels believers when they are walking through difficult seasons!

The Holy Spirit Wills Believers to Go Forward and Witness about Christ

The Holy Spirit supernaturally empowers believers to do the work of witnessing. Their sealing and filling should result in a willingness to be available to do whatever God calls them to do—which should be more than just shouts of conviction! Don't forget: Paul declared that when a person believes in Jesus Christ they "shall receive power, after that the Holy Ghost is come upon you: and ye shall be witnesses unto me both in Jerusalem, and in all Judaea, and in Samaria, and unto the uttermost part of the earth" (Acts 1:8 KJV).

Goals to Aspire to as a Christian

Because of this gift of the Holy Spirit and this power available to all who believe; the church should aspire to reflect certain characteristics. Believers should possess a grateful heart for others and be excited about sharing Jesus. They may not have a dime, but sharing Jesus with another person is free and the benefit it priceless!

Consider the lame man's response when he was healed: he started walking, jumping, and praising. Not only was he glad about his healing but he also praised God on his own—and the people around him were filled with amazement. He became a literal walking testimony to what God had done in his life, and the message of the gospel continued to spread. This is how the mission of the church is accomplished.

The power released when God's people trust Him will not only impact those close to them, but it will fuel the evangelism movement beyond what can be imagined.

CHAPTER FOUR

The Power Resisted

Acts 4

And when they had prayed, the place was shaken where they were assembled together; and they were all filled with the Holy Ghost, and they spake the word of God with boldness. And the multitude of them that believed were of one heart and of one soul: neither said any of them that ought of the things which he possessed was his own; but they had all things common. And with great power gave the apostles witness of the resurrection of the Lord Jesus: and great grace was upon them all. — Acts 4:31–33 (KJV)

Each chapter of Acts reveals the Holy Spirit working and winning in the early church. By Acts 4, the church movement had reached a new high because many of the people who heard the apostles' message believed it. The movement had grown to five thousand. However, whenever there is a move of God, Satan is close behind; he will do everything possible to stop God's Kingdom from being advanced. As the disciples gained new victories and the church movement grew, Satan's plan to pull out the road blocks was in full forces.

Peter and John had attracted a crowd after the lame man picked up his bed and walked. They were amazed at Peter, who said, "Why marvel ye at this? or why look ye so earnestly on us, as though by our own power or holiness we had made this man to walk?" (Acts 3:12 KJV). It wasn't Peter who healed the lame man, but the Holy Spirit through Peter.

Peter exhorted the people who had witnessed the miracle to "that your sins may be blotted out, when the times of refreshing shall come from the presence of the Lord" (Acts 3:19 KJV). The miracle happened not by Peter's might, but by the power of the Holy Spirit.

The religious leaders were angered that Peter and John had been preaching about Jesus Christ being raised from the dead. They were even more incensed that Peter and John had gained the attention of such large crowds. In the middle of their preaching, the chief priests, the captain of the temple police, and some of the Sadducees came over to them and arrested them. It was already evening so they jailed Peter and John overnight—before not before the word got out of the miracle that had occurred! The movement had reached a new high because many of the people who had heard their message believed it. The movement had grown to five thousand.

Church Movements Invites Resistance

Any movement is likely to meet disapproval from others. In most cases, it is because the issue at hand comes against a person's moral, political, or spiritual view. In the case of the early church, the problem was rooted in the hearts of those who should have been the most welcoming to the Jesus, their Savior—the religious leaders.

The Problem

The religious leaders were angry at Peter and John, "grieved that that they taught the people, and preached through Jesus the resurrection from the dead" (Acts 4:2 KJV). They could not make sense of the fact that this message caused so many people to believe in Jesus (Acts 1:4). Rather than humbly coming before Peter and John to dig a little deeper and find out if what they claimed was true, they "laid hands on them, and put them in hold unto the next day," (Acts 4:3 KJV) arresting them.

The religious leaders knew whom Jesus had claimed to be; they were not unaware that God was their Savior, for throughout the Old Testament Scriptures, God had reminded them, "I, even I, am the LORD; and beside me there is no saviour" (Isaiah 43:11 KJV), and "There is no God else beside me; a just God and a Saviour" (Isaiah 45:21–22 KJV). Jesus had ruffled the religious leaders' feathers by claiming to be God; He was a threat to their religious system and way of life. This is often why people come against Christianity. It's not that they don't know they have a deep need for forgiveness, but that they don't want to have to change their current way of life or their moral, political or spiritual views.

And so, Peter and John were arrested—but not before the gospel was preached. The relgious leaders were too late. Five thousand men were added to the church that day (Acts 4:4) adding to the three thousand that had been saved on the day of Pentecost.

The power of the Holy Spirit cannot be contained! When the church steps out in obedience as witnesses for Christ, His power does what mere man cannot.

The Resisters

Peter and John spent a night in jail and the next day were brought before their accusers at a gathering of the Sanhedrin council. These scholars, dignitaries and religious elite were assembled with one main purpose in mind: to intimidate Peter and John for what they had said and done.

An impressive crowd of religious leaders had gathered in Acts 4:5–6. Make note of Luke's eight uses of the word 'and' in just two verses:

> And it came to pass on the morrow, that their rulers, and elders, and scribes, And Annas the high priest, and Caiaphas, and John, and Alexander, and as many as were of the kindred of the high priest, were gathered together at Jerusalem. — *Acts 4:5–6 (KJV)*

Repetition of the word 'and' is a literary technique called a *polysyndeton*. *Polysyndeton* is often "employed as a tool to lay emphasis to the ideas the conjunctions connect."[17] Thus, Luke (the writer of Acts) was emphasizing how many key religious leaders came against Peter and John.

The revolt was led by the proud, esteemed high priest Annas, as well as the Sadducees. The Sadducees were a key Jewish sect in New Testament times. They were aristocratic, wealthy, and influential. The high priest was usually chosen from their ranks. The Sadducees' theology denied the supernatural, the existence of spirits, and the possibility of a resurrection. They led the nation in rejection of Christ.

The Sadducees were in a vulnerable position because Jesus' resurrection had disproved their theology. Rather than confess they were wrong, they took the lead in persecuting the church. According to John Philips in his book *Exploring Acts,* "The Pharisees as recorded in the gospels fomented the rejection of Christ; in Acts the Sadducees lead it."[18]

The high priest Annas protested against *where* Peter had been preaching and the Sadducees protested because of *what* Peter had been preaching.

Probing and the Power

These angry religious leaders immediately asked Peter and John the big question: "By what power, or by what name, have ye done this?" (Acts 4:7 KJV). Peter was probably thinking to himself, "You couldn't have asked me a better question!"

Peter, filled with the Holy Spirit, began to preach...while in chains. The Message Bible translates this passage of Peter preaching under the power of the Holy Spirit as follows:

> *With that, Peter, full of the Holy Spirit, let loose: "Rulers and leaders of the people, if we have been brought to trial today for helping a sick man, put under investigation regarding this healing, I'll be completely frank with you— we have nothing to hide. By the name of Jesus Christ of Nazareth, the One you killed on a cross, the One God raised from the dead, by means of his name this man stands before you healthy and whole. Jesus is 'the stone you masons threw out, which is now the cornerstone.' Salvation comes no other way; no other name has been or will be given to us by which we can be saved, only this one."* — *Acts 4:8–12 (MSG)*

Enabled by the power of the Holy Spirit to be a witness to those religious leaders, Acts 4:8 says Peter "let loose" (MSG) He boldly declared the person and work of Jesus Christ, and the way to salvation. This is the message all Christians are called to declare!

The Apostles' Persuasion

The interrogators saw something in Peter and John that exceeded their expectations. They percieved these two men to be ignorant, awkard and even slow of learning until they began to speak with clarity and boldness because of the empowerment of the Holy Spirit.

At that point, the religious leaders concluded Peter and John had clearly spent time with Jesus. Peter and John were standing in the impressive surroundings of the richest, most educated, noblest, and most powerful men of their day; they were "out of their league!" However, when Peter finished speaking, there was no doubt, even in the minds of the trained religious leaders that Peter had been on point with every scripture. Luke wrote, "Now when they [the religious leaders] saw the boldness of Peter and John, and perceived that they were unlearned and ignorant men, they marvelled; and they took knowledge of them, that they had been with Jesus" (Acts 4:13 KJV, clarification added). Peter had dissected the Scriptures like a surgeon and presented a sound theological argument of which the religious leaders "could say nothing against" (Acts 4:14 KJV).

These two were considered common men who by most people's estimation should have been begging for forgiveness with their heads hung low. But their actions reflected the exact opposite. They stood, unapologetic and unashamed, persuading their audience of the Lordship of Christ by the leading of the Spirit as ambassadors from the royal city of Heaven.

Holy Spirit Power Cannot Be Stopped

The council was dumbfounded, speechless because living evidence was standing in front of them: the lame man was visibly healed. Peter and John attributed his healing to the power of Jesus' name; there was no way they could prove otherwise. These men were at a loss for words, so they decided to break the session to try to regroup and said, "What shall we do to these men? for that indeed a notable miracle hath been done by them is manifest to all them that dwell in Jerusalem; and we cannot deny it" (Acts 4:16 KJV).

Not knowing what to do, they sent the apostles away to try and think of a strategy. They knew that a miracle had taken place and they could not deny it. But these religious leaders were more concerned about the possibility of damaging their religious reputations than the truth of Peter and John's words, so they decided they would threaten Peter and John to keep them quiet and commanded them "not to speak at all nor teach in the name of Jesus" (Acts 4:18 KJV).

The religious leaders called Peter and John back into the session. I imagine they put on their meanest and most intimidating faces and voices and said to the two apostles, "Now look! Don't say another word about Jesus or you will be in big trouble and we mean it!" But Peter and John continued speaking, declaring:

> *Whether it be right in the sight of God to hearken unto you more than unto God, judge ye. For we cannot but speak the things which we have seen and heard.* — *Acts 4:19–20 (KJV)*

With no other plan, the leaders "further threatened them" (Acts 4:21 KJV) and let them go. They could offer nothing but threats against the two apostles because the people had personally witnessed the miracle and were already glorifying and praising God. The church movement was already strong and those leaders knew they would incite a riot if they came against it. The power of the Holy Spirit dwelling within God's people cannot be stopped!

As soon as Peter and John were released they returned to their church family and began to share their testimony and all that the Sanhedrin had threatened them with. After hearing all that had happened, these faithful followers—the first church—held a prayer meeting, all praying the same with one accord. "Lord, behold their threatenings," they asked of God: "...and grant unto thy servants, that with all boldness they may speak thy word" (Acts 4:29 KJV). Rather than shrinking back in fear, they sought the Lord and asked for more power to continue doing the work of the gospel!

So too should God's people today. There will be resistance to the gospel; people will come against any movement of God, and target God's people as His representatives. Perhaps this is why James so boldly exhorted believers, "Resist the devil, and he will flee from you." (James 4:7 KJV) Push through resistance to the gospel, for "greater is he that is in you, than he that is in the world" (1 John 4:4 KJV). His power will prevail.

God's Power Prevails

When the disciples finished praying, the Holy Ghost moved within their presence as He did on the day of Pentecost. The place they were gathered in was shaken, they were all filled with the power of the Spirit of God, and they proceeded to speak with boldness. The only major difference was there was no speaking of tongues. Why? There were no foriegners present which proves tongues were a language and a gift given for the sole purpose of spreading the gospel to people that did not speak the same language.

At the end of Acts 4, Luke describes a group of Jesus followers who as a collective group was united as one. Everyone had one heart and one mind and one destination; they were not selfish with their belongings, "but they had all things common" (Acts 4:32 KJV). The fledgling church included members who were good stewards over their time, talents and treasures—many selling possessions for the furthering of the Kingdom; no one went without (Acts 4:34).

The apostles kept preaching about the resurrected Jesus and witnessed of Jesus continuously and God's "great grace was upon them all" (Acts 4:33 KJV).

Movements pull people forward and perplex power structures. The Holy Spirit brings a supernatural confidence that results in God's Word going out and stirring people to consider the truth of the gospel.

What is the key? The disciples had spent time with Jesus. So too much the church if it is to continue the movement that began in the first century. Spending time with Jesus makes the difference in how one may be used in unimaginable ways by the Holy Spirit to witness. The disciples had clear standing and tangible evidence standing by their side of unusual power; so do believers today. Each person's story of transformation is evidence of the work of God, and no one can argue against it.

The gospel changes lives. God is inviting believers to something greater than themselves—a movement that involves bringing people from a place of death, to life.

Are you ready to be part of the greatest movement in history?

CHAPTER FIVE

Protecting the Integrity of the Church

Acts 5

And now I say unto you, Refrain from these men, and let them alone: for if this counsel or this work be of men, it will come to nought: But if it be of God, ye cannot overthrow it; lest haply ye be found even to fight against God. And to him they agreed: and when they had called the apostles, and beaten them, they commanded that they should not speak in the name of Jesus, and let them go. —
Acts 5:38–40 (KJV)

The Holy Spirit is active in the movement of the church, but believers cannot effectively take a stand for Jesus until they have been filled with the Holy Spirit. When this happens, the believer is equipped to complete every good work. However, good work for Christ is not without opposition. Faith in God does not make troublemakers go away. However, God is not unaware, and will send help from unexpected people, places and things to assist the church in accomplishing His work. In fact, the Holy Spirit is ready to counter opposition before it occurs!

Prepare for Opposition

Opposition comes from two places: outside of the movement and from inside the movement. In Acts 4, Peter had been fighting *outside* opposition from the Jewish leaders who desperately made an attempt to prohibit the movement of the church. Now, at the beginning of Acts 5, Luke described the Holy Spirit protecting the church from *inside* opposition that had manifested in the form of hypocrisy and deceitfulness. Unfortunately, opposition from within causes much more damage than opposition from the outside.

The problem facing the movement in Acts 5 was a couple named Ananias and Sapphira whose act of monetary giving was with a hypocritical heart. Back in Acts 4:32–35, the Bible is clear that first century believers shared everything, and had all things in common. They sold their properties, possessions and brought money and laid it at the apostles' feet to be distributed to those in need.

One of the generous givers noted in the closing verses of the Acts 4 was Barnabas, who would later travel with Paul. Acts 4:37 tells how Barnabis sold land that he owned and gave it to the apostles for the benefit of the Kingdom. After he had offered his gift, Ananias and

Sapphira decided to give a similar gift—but their motives were less than honorable.

A Couple Defiled

Ananias and his wife, Sapphira, were a married couple who came together and planned take advantage of the church but in doing so offended the Holy Spirit. The couple conspired together to sell a piece of land but secretly kept part of the money and bringing the rest to the apostles as an offering. They appeared to be generous givers, making what looked like a full sacrifice, while they were in reality lying.

This may have been an attempt to impress others because the two came forward to make their gift after Barnabas had made his. Ananias and Sapphira were not forced to give anything—so why did they lie?

At least three common sins can be seen in the couple's decision to lie: pride, dishonesty, and greed.

Pride

Barnabas's gift in Acts was a gift that did not go unnoticed. He probably received a lot of accolades for his gift, but his offering was an outpouring of his love for God—not an attempt at gaining attention. His heart was in the right place and he was committed to the work of Jesus Christ.

Ananias and Sapphira's gift on the other hand stemmed from pride; they wanted attention and praise and were not concerned about the work of the movement of the gospel. They wanted the spotlight.

Dishonesty

Ananias and Sapphira wanted their gift to appear more sacrificial then it really was. Others had sold their land and given the whole price of sale to the church but these two held back a portion. They gave the impression that they gave all of the proceeds but they lied about their giving.

Greed

Finally, Ananias and Sapphira were more concerned about the things of this world and not the things of God. Why did they hold back a portion of their money? Greed. It is no secret that advancement costs money and the early church needed money. Yet there are people that always hold back what they can give to help because of greed.

Pride, dishonesty, and greed are sins that will sink their claws into the church will dramatically slow the movement of the gospel down.

A Lie unto God

The couple lied to the apostles, but more disheartingly, they lied to God, and they could not keep the secret for long. Peter exposed the couple. Peter said, "Ananias, why hath Satan filled thine heart to lie to the

Holy Ghost, and to keep back part of the price of the land? ...Thou hast not lied unto men, but unto God." (Acts 5:4–5 KJV).

John 16:13 teaches that the Holy Spirit guides followers of Jesus into all truth, and Paul said God will "bring to light the hidden things of darkness, and will make manifest the counsels of the hearts" (1 Corinthians 4:5 KJV). The Holy Spirit revealed Ananias's sin to Peter (but Scripture does not give the details of how); sin will always find a person out (Numbers 32:23) and in Ananias' case, his sin caught up with him rather quickly.

Imagine Ananias's response when Peter asked Him why he had lied to the Holy Ghost. "How does he know?" he must have thought. His secret was laid bare for everyone in the church to know, just as the apostle Luke affirmed in Luke 8:17: "For nothing is secret, that shall not be made manifest; neither any thing hid, that shall not be known and come abroad" (KJV).

Ananais's little secret did not remain between him and his wife as he had hoped. He had no idea that the Holy Spirit knew their deceiftful plan, and brought their dark sin into the light.

The Holy Spirit gives God's people the ability to discern truth from error. The prophet Hosea declared that the "ways of the LORD are right, and the just shall walk in them" (Hosea 14:9 KJV). By the leading of the Holy Spirit Peter discerned the couple's lie. Those who walk close to the Lord will be given the supernatural ability to discern what others are not capable of discerning.

Rather than being lifted up and acknowledged for their amazing gift, they were shot down. Ananais had brought his gift first, while Sapphira brought hers three hours later. Perhaps the two were hoping to prolong the anticipated praise they thought they would receive from the people. If Ananias came first they would praise him and when Sapphirra shows up three hours later (fashionably late) she would receive applause as well.

This was not the case: Peter immediately denounced their deceitful actions.

Scripture reveals the consequence for lying to the Holy Spirit was harsh. After Peter denounced Ananais for his sin, Luke wrote that Ananais "fell down, and gave up the ghost" (Acts 5:5 KJV). He died, and fear enveloped those who heard what happened. When Sapphira showed up with her offering, she fell down and died as well (Acts 5:10).

Ananias and Sapphira's story is both a warning and a consolation that God will protect His church from not only external enemies, but internal ones as well.

A Purified and Magnified Church

From this deceitful couple, Scripture teaches God wants to both purify and magnify His church. Their deaths were so shocking the Bible says "great fear came upon all the church" (Acts 5:11 KJV).

The phrase "great fear" indicates fear that promotes righteousness. Ananais and Sapphira's immediate deaths taught the disciples the importance of living an upright life, and how it directly impacts the purity to the church. Though a sad story, this object lesson made the church more powerful.

God also desires to magnify His church. Those in the community outside the church also experienced great fear because of the shock of this judgment (Acts 5:11). As a result, "the people magnified them [the church]" (Acts 5:13, KJV clarification added). To 'magnify' is the Greek word *megalynō,* which means "to make or declare great, to get the glory and praise."[19] Those who watched what happened to Ananais and Sapphira were drawn to the church, giving it glory and praise.

The providential hand of the Holy Spirit moves within the fully committed church to counter opposition, so that it will be purified and magnified to a watching world. The result will be a fresh boldness that will sometimes invite more and stronger opposition. But with the power of the Holy Spirit, the church will be equipped with everything needed to fight even the toughest battles.

The Explosion of Miracles and the Multitude of Members

Great fear had came over the church because of Ananias and Sapphira's dishonesty that ultimately led to their death. After their death, God began to use signs and wonders through the apostles to point people to the gospel message. As a result, many people joined the church. These signs and wonders (miracles) validated the apostles' gospel message and caused people to believe God. Consider the following verses:

> *Through mighty signs and wonders, by the power of the Spirit of God; so that from Jerusalem, and round about*

unto Illyricum, I have fully preached the gospel of Christ.
— **Romans 15:19 (KJV)**

*Long time therefore abode they speaking boldly in the
Lord, which gave testimony unto the word of his grace, and
granted signs and wonders to be done by their hands.*
— *Acts 14:3 (KJV)*

*Then all the multitude kept silence, and gave audience to
Barnabas and Paul, declaring what miracles and wonders
God had wrought among the Gentiles by them.* — *Acts
15:12 (KJV)*

God still works wonders today. However, the need for
confirming miracles has passed. The Word of God is
available in a way it was not available for the first
century apostles. Believers can test teachers by their
message, corroborating it with God's Word, not their
miracles, just as the Bereans did who "searched the
scriptures daily, whether those things were so" (Acts
17:11 KJV).

Angelic Assistance

But the outside opposition didn't stop. When the high
priest and the Sadducees learned of these signs and
wonders and the resulting growing movement of the
church, they rose up and arrested the apostles, throwing
them in prison (Acts 5:17–18). The only thing the
apostles were guilty of was preaching and teaching about
Jesus Christ. The Jewish leaders questioned their mission

and opposed them every step of the way. (Acts 5:17–28, 33).

But God sent an angel to deliver them from their jail cell. Luke wrote that the angel of the Lord came at night and opened the prison doors, brought them out and said, "Go, stand and speak in the temple to the people all the words of this life" (Acts 5:20 KJV). This theme of angelic assistance is woven throughout the book of Acts.

Nothing will stop the movement of the church when it's members step out in the power of the Spirit as witnesses.

Inward Boldness and Unexpected Help

As the angel instructed, the apostles went straight back into the temple and began to teach the very next morning. Immediately, the high priest pounded the apostles with questions:

> *Did not we straitly command you that ye should not teach in this name? and, behold, ye have filled Jerusalem with your doctrine, and intend to bring this man's blood upon us. Then Peter and the other apostles answered and said, We ought to obey God rather than men. The God of our fathers raised up Jesus, whom ye slew and hanged on a tree. Him hath God exalted with his right hand to be a Prince and a Saviour, for to give repentance to Israel, and forgiveness of sins. And we are his witnesses of these things; and so is also the Holy Ghost, whom God hath given to them that obey him.* — *Acts 5:28–32 (KJV)*

When the religious leaders heard the apostles preaching the gospel, Scripture says, they were "cut to the heart, and took counsel to slay them" (Acts 5:33 KJV) when an unexpected ally stepped in. His name was Gamaliel. Gamaliel was a respected Pharisee and teacher of the law (Acts 5:34) who is best known in the Bible for training the apostle Paul.

Gamaliel convinced the council from harming the apostles saying:

> *Refrain from these men, and let them alone: for if this counsel or this work be of men, it will come to nought: But if it be of God, ye cannot overthrow it; lest haply ye be found even to fight against God.* — *Acts 5:38–39 (KJV)*

The council subsequently released the disciple, but not before beating them and commanding them not to speak in the name of Jesus.

Nonetheless, they continued the practice of teaching which proved critical to the movement. Their preaching was insistent, consistent, and bold ... and the movement continued.

Opposition to the gospel is inevitable, and sometimes it may seem like God is absent; however, the Holy Spirit has already made plans to counter opposition when it comes. Sometimes opposition comes from outside influences, like the religious leaders in the first century. Today, it may come in the form of boycotts, discrimination in work environments, punishment for stands on moral beliefs, or even isolation.

Remember that Jesus warned believers ahead of time they would face persecution. He knew opposition would come from within the church and outside of the church, saying, "If the world hate you, ye know that it hated me before it hated you" (John 15:18 KJV). When inside the church, God will discipline (sometimes harshly!) to keep His church pure and magnified. When opposition comes from outside of the church, God will be faithful and show up in the believer's time of need. Stand firm and wait for the unexpected help for it will come.

CHAPTER SIX

The Source of All Strength

Acts 6

And all that sat in the council, looking stedfastly on him, saw his face as it had been the face of an angel. — *Acts 6:15 (KJV)*

The promise of power was given in Acts 1, the power was received in Acts 2, the power was presented in Acts 3, the power was resisted in Acts 4, and the power protected the integrity of the church in Acts 5.

Now, in Acts 6, God's Holy Spirit is revealed through His power as an organizer, and as the source of all strength.

As the first century church grew, God established His intended structure and provided strength to the believers when they faced opposition. There are some that reject structure and believe the church should flow in the Spirit. Others believe the church should be run like a corporation and want to extricate the Holy Spirit from any part of governing. The church is not a public park where anything goes, neither is it an organization bound by restrictive structures. It is an organism, a living body, where all of the members are connected to one head— Jesus Christ—and led by the Holy Spirit.

The early church functioned orderly when each member knew their role and carried it out according to the dictates of the Holy Spirit. But as the church movement grew, organization was required. Someone kept count of the membership; church members met at specific times and at specific locations. Money was collected and distributed to those in need. Teaching was intentional and systematic. The church responded to needs as the Holy Spirit directed.

The church faced its first organizational dilemma in Acts 6, but the Holy Spirit responded. The disciples increased in number and fullness of Spirit, and the church expanded.

The Demands of a Growing Church

The last count of the church was five thousand in Acts 4:4 and that number only included the men. Counting women and children it is not a stretch to suggest the church had expanded to twenty thousand. As a consequence, the twelve apostles could no longer meet the demands of the growing church. The Grecian (Hellenistic) Jews began to complain that their widows were being overlooked in the daily distribution of food, "neglected in the daily ministration" (Acts 6:1 KJV). It is likely they felt this neglect was deliberate and that racism played a part.

God's Organizational Structure

The leaders of the church recognized the problem and called the multitude before them and said, "It is not reason that we should leave the word of God, and serve tables" (Acts 6:2 KJV). These leaders acknowledged they did not have time to handle the problem because their primary role was to deliver the Word of God. To do both would divide their time and their focus. Therefore, they would not leave the Word of God to serve tables.

Today, pastors are bogged down with responsibilities that reach beyond their call to train others in the Word of God. They would do well to heed the early church leader's example, and focus solely on "the perfecting of the saints, for the work of the ministry, for the edifying of the body of Christ" (Ephesians 4:12 KJV).

The apostles commanded the believers to select seven men of good reputation, full of the Holy Spirit and wisdom (Acts 6:3), to serve as deacons. Though the word 'deacon' is not mentioned directly in Acts 6, it does show up in Paul's writing. Consider Philippians 1:1 and 1 Timothy 3:8–13:

*Paul and Timotheus, the servants of Jesus Christ, to all the saints in Christ Jesus which are at Philippi, with the bishops and deacons. — **Philippians 1:1 (KJV)***

Likewise must the deacons be grave, not doubletongued, not given to much wine, not greedy of filthy lucre; Holding the mystery of the faith in a pure conscience.

And let these also first be proved; then let them use the office of a deacon, being found blameless. Even so must their wives be grave, not slanderers, sober, faithful in all things. Let the deacons be the husbands of one wife, ruling their children and their own houses well. For they that have used the office of a deacon well purchase to themselves a good degree, and great boldness in the faith which is in Christ Jesus. — 1 Timothy 3:8–13 (KJV)

The English word 'deacon' comes from the Greek word *diakonos*, which means "one who executes the commands of another, especially that of a master, servant, attendant or minister."[20] The deacon was one of two offices established to help organize the church—the other being the office of pastor.

The deacon's role was to work alongside the pastor to assure church members' needs were met. The twelve apostles called members of the congregation to "look ye out among you seven men of honest report, full of the Holy Ghost and wisdom, *whom we may appoint over this business*" in (Acts 6:3 (KJV), emphasis added). However, the apostles would make the final decision regarding each deacon's appointment, as indicated by the words "whom we may appoint over the business" Acts 6:3 KJV) while we continue to pray and study God's Word.

There has been great debate over this verse. Some feel the church is responsible for selecting deacons and not the pastor. To help interpret this scripture accurately, consider the Old Testament account of selecting leaders to assist leaders in Exodus 18. Here Scripture portrays a similar situation as in Acts 6. Moses needed help for the weighty responsibility He had to care for the nation of Israel:

> *Moses chose able men out of all Israel, and made them heads over the people, rulers of thousands, rulers of hundreds, rulers of fifties, and rulers of tens. And they judged the people at all seasons: the hard causes they brought unto Moses, but every small matter they judged themselves. And Moses let his father in law depart; and he went his way into his own land.* — ***Exodus 18:25–27 (KJV)***

Moses set the precedent thousands of years before the apostles walked this earth for who should select deacons; Moses chose the men he felt could best assist him. So, too, should pastors.

The apostles' plan "pleased the whole multitude" (Acts 6:5 KJV). The men selected as deacons were Greek Jews, thereby thwarting Satan's attempt to use racial tension to divide the church.

Acts 6 then describes what would later become God's ordination process for the church. After setting the seven prospective deacons before the apostles, the apostles prayed and "laid their hands on them" (Acts 6:6 KJV).

Luke closed this section, as he had before, by noting the further development of the church. The Word of God continued to spread because the apostles were at liberty to carry out their primary ministry of the Word. As the Word continued the number of the disciples increased.

Finally, "a great company of the priests were obedient to the faith" (Acts 6:7 KJV). These were not the chief priests or members of the Sanhedrin, but a very large number of the rank and file priests who ministered in the temple.

The church today needs organization for the same reasons as the early church. Pastors must be free to focus on prayer, preaching and teaching the Word. Better organization can help meet the needs of all members and avoid conflict.

The Holy Spirit was the driving force that established the organizational structure of the early church. The Spirit produced the apostles' awareness of the situation but also directed their steps in finding a solution through a process of selection. This satisfied the church who sealed the selection of the new deacons with a public presentation—their "ordination."

When human leaders try to establish an organizational structure within a church as if is were a corporate business, it will flounder. The church is God's, and He knows perfectly how it should operate.

The Holy Spirit as the Source of the Believer's Strength

Under the guidance of the Holy Spirit and the apostles' leadership, and with the deacon's assistance, the church aggressively forged ahead. Stephen, one of the deacons the apostles had selected, demonstrated how the Holy Spirit poured out unusual power to supplement the believer's weaknesses with boldness beyond belief.

Luke wrote in Acts 6:8 that Stephen, "full of faith and power, did great wonders and miracles among the people" (KJV). The phrase 'full of faith' was also used a few verses earlier in Acts 6:5 to describe Stephen.

To be 'full' in Acts 6:5 and 8 is the Greek word *plērēs* which means "to be full, filled up, or complete."[21] Paul used a derivative of the same word in Ephesians 5:18 when he said, "And be not drunk with wine, wherein is excess; but be filled (*plēroō*) with the Spirit" (KJV).

Stephen was thus filled up (complete) with the Spirit, lacking nothing. Stephen did great wonders and miracles among the people. He trusted God to carry out his individual assignment of being a witness for Jesus Christ. His fullness of faith resulted in a fullness of power. He continually made an impact on those he came in contact with. He was open to the Holy Spirit to move in his life. Believers who trust God and are committed to Him as His witnesses will be filled to completeness, too, with the power of God's Spirit. They will lack nothing!

The Attack Against the Anointing

Some men rose up against Stephen, but Scripture says they were not able to resist the wisdom and the Spirit by which Stephen spoke:

> *Then there arose certain of the synagogue, which is called the synagogue of the Libertines, and Cyrenians, and Alexandrians, and of them of Cilicia and of Asia, disputing with Stephen. And they were not able to resist the wisdom and the spirit by which he spake. — Acts 6:9–10 (KJV)*

Men from at least three different Jewish synagogues disputed Stephen, angry because Stephen taught against Jewish tradition. But their human argument was no contest for Stephen's God-given abilities. They accused Stephen of speaking blasphemous words against Moses and against God (Acts 6:11), which "stirred up the people, and the elders, and the scribes" who "came upon him, and caught him, and brought him to the council (Acts 6:12). They even set up false witnesses against Stephen who testified that Stephen never stopped speaking blasphemous words against the temple ("this holy place") and the law (Acts 6:13).

The attack appeared to be against Stephen, but in reality it was against his anointing—the Holy Spirit. John 15:18 says, "If the world hates you, keep in mind that it hated me first" (NIV). The church and its members will be attacked and may even be charged with false testimony; however, they must stand firm to the truth of who is really being attacked and press on.

The Consolation for the Christian

At this point in Acts, something unexplainable happened to Stephen. "And all that sat in the council, looking steadfastly on him, saw his face as it had been the face of an angel" (Acts 6:15 KJV).

Adam Clark's commentary on the Bible describes this phrase "fact of an angel" as follows:

This expression is one evidently denoting that he manifested evidence of sincerity, gravity, fearlessness, confidence in God. It is used in the Old Testament to denote peculiar wisdom (2 Samuel 14:17; 19:27). In Genesis 33:10, it is used to denote peculiar majesty and glory, as if it were the face of God. When Moses came down from Mount Sinai from communing with God, it is said that the skin of his face shone, so that the children of Israel were afraid to come near him (Exodus 34:29, 30; 2 Corinthians 3:7, 13; compare Revelation 1:16 and Matthew 17:2).[22]

In the Bible, 'light' or 'fire' is often associated with the presence of God, as seen in the pillar (or cloud) of fire the Israelites followed in the wilderness: "By day the LORD went ahead of them in a pillar of cloud to guide them on their way and by night in a pillar of fire to give them light, so that they could travel by day or night" (Exodus 13:21 NIV). When being accused by the religious leaders, Stephen didn't stutter or tremble but only radiated the glory, or the presence, of God.

This concept shows up repeatedly in the Bible. For example, Moses' face shone when he came down from Mount Sinai (Exodus 34:35). Christ's face shone on the Mount of Transfiguration (Matthew 17:2). The Jews say of Phineas that when the Holy Ghost was upon him, his face burned or shone like a torch.[23] And Stephen was now full of the Holy Ghost—radiating God's presence to those who were watching, described as an angelic face. Those who trust God will be filled with God's presence, too—people will notice, and the movement of the church will continue.

How to Respond under Persecution

Opposition and even persecution was inevitable for the early church. The gospel makes people uncomfortable, because it forces them to consider their own moral compass. When persecution comes, remember the Holy Spirit that dwells within believers will pour out the ability to withstand anything.

Trust the Holy Spirit to give a spirit of calmness. Though Stephen was accused of blasphemy he remained quiet. God promises in Isaiah 26:3 He will give believers peace if they trust in Him: "Thou wilt keep him in perfect peace, whose mind is stayed on thee: because he trusteth in thee" (KJV).

Also, trust the Holy Spirit to instill confidence. Stephen was able to speak with the authority of God only because it was the Holy Spirit speaking through him. Paul affirmed in Philippians 4:13, "I can do all things through Christ which strengtheneth me" (KJV).

Finally, trust the Holy Spirit to counter enemies. The Holy Spirit will turn adversaries' weapons on them. God answered the religious leaders' charges by putting His glory on Stephen. God never left Stephen just as He never left Moses in the Old Testament—and He will never leave you, either.

God always works on His people's behalf. The Chronicler wrote, "And he said, Hearken ye, all Judah, and ye inhabitants of Jerusalem, and thou king Jehoshaphat, Thus saith the LORD unto you, Be not afraid nor dismayed by reason of this great multitude; for the battle is not yours, but God's" (2 Chronicles 20:15 KJV).

In similar language, noted gospel singer Richard Smallwood's powerful song "Total Praise" includes the following lyrics:

> Lord I will lift my eyes to the hills knowing my help is coming from you. Your peace you give me in time of the storm. You are the source of my strength; you are the strength of my life. I lift my hands in total praise to you.[24]

As the church movement grew, organization was required. God established His intended structure and provided strength to the believers when they faced opposition. It was a lesson for the disciples in trusting God's leading through the power of His Holy Spirit to make the decisions. So too did Stephen trust in the Holy Spirit—not for making decisions, but for peace while in the battle and for strength to speak truth. God's Spirit will always show up as both organizer of the church, and strength for its members' lives.

CHAPTER SEVEN

Production Through Persecution

Acts 7

But he, being full of the Holy Ghost, looked up stedfastly into heaven, and saw the glory of God, and Jesus standing on the right hand of God, And said, Behold, I see the heavens opened, and the Son of man standing on the right hand of God. Then they cried out with a loud voice, and stopped their ears, and ran upon him with one accord, And cast him out of the city, and stoned him: and the witnesses laid down their clothes at a young man's feet, whose name was Saul. And they stoned Stephen, calling upon God, and saying, Lord Jesus, receive my spirit. — Acts 7:55–59 (KJV)

Acts 6 described Stephen as being full of faith. While being attacked by the crowd the Holy Spirit's anointing fell on Stephen, consoling him and physically changing his appearance. Although there were people that opposed Stephen and accused him, God allowed His glory to be revealed in the appearance of his face, confirming Stephen's witness, in spite of the persecution.

The priest next gave Stephen an opportunity to speak and his response became the longest sermon in Acts. It contained a history lesson on the Old Testament. This fifty-verse sermon is like the Old Testament in miniature form. Then, in Acts 7, the Bible documents the first Christian martyr—one who died for the cause of the gospel. Though hard to understand, the persecution of the saints is not without purpose.

The Testimony of the Word of God

Stephen began affirming to the high priest that indeed he had preached the blasphemous things he had been accused of. But he did not miss the opportunity to speak and convince more people of the messiahship of Jesus. He began with history of God's people with the call of Abraham and how God honored Abraham's faith, saying:

> *And he said, Men, brethren, and fathers, hearken; The God of glory appeared unto our father Abraham, when he was in Mesopotamia, before he dwelt in Charran, And said unto him, Get thee out of thy country, and from thy kindred, and come into the land which I shall shew thee.* — *Acts 7:2–3 (KJV)*

When Abraham obeyed God and left his country of birth, a movement began. Abraham's descendants, the tribes of Israel—who eventually established the kingdom of Israel—were literally the foundation of how God's people expanded into a great nation. Included were the patriarchal stories of Joseph and Moses. Genesis reveals the patriarchal men in the Bible were instrumental in the faith.

The leaders that listened to Stephen's account could not refute what they heard because they were well versed in their own history. They were condemned as Stephen reminded them every leader God had sent Israel had been rejected. He mentioned Joseph and Moses because Israel rejected them both. Joseph was turned over to gentiles and Moses was rejected as a judge and a leader.

The weight of Stephen's argument was to make the Jews' rejection of God's Redeemer of Israel, Jesus Christ, apparent to the those listening. In verse 37 Stephen reminded his audience that thousands of years prior Moses had foretold, "A prophet shall the Lord your God raise up unto you of your brethren, like unto me" (Acts 7:37 KJV). A unique Jewish prophet *like* Moses would minister to His own people, who would reject Him. Then, Stephen reminded them that Israel had also rejected the prophets themselves that testified to, or pointed to Jesus. "Which of the prophets have not your fathers persecuted? and they have slain them which shewed before of the coming of the Just One; of whom ye have been now the betrayers and murderers," he said in (Acts 7:52 KJV).

Stephen used the Jewish leaders' Hebrew Scriptures to point out what they already knew well; Jews of the time knew their Scriptures inside and out. The witness to Christ came straight from the Word of God. Stephen reminded the Jews that though they had the presence of the living God dwelling among them while wandering in the desert, they had slipped into idolatry, worshipping a golden calf instead of God—the work of their own hands (Acts 7:41) as well as Moloch and "the star of your god, Remphan, figures which ye made to worship them" (Acts 7:43 KJV).

When the people heard these things, Scripture says, "they were cut to the heart, and they gnashed on him with their teeth" (Acts 7:54 KJV). They knew what Stephen said was true.

Opposing the Holy Spirit

To 'resist' in the original Greek is the word *antipiptō*, which means "to run against, to be opposed or to strive against."[25] Thus, to resist the Holy Spirit literally means to oppose Him.

Israel had always resisted the work of the Holy Spirit, and it had even prevented them from entering the Promised Land and being the witness to the world God intended. "Ye stiffnecked and uncircumcised in heart and ears, ye do always resist the Holy Ghost: as your fathers did, so do ye," Stephen accused! Though Stephen presented God's truth, they continued to harden their hearts (Acts 7:51 KJV).

Unlike the religious leaders of the day and their ancestors who lived thousands of years before them, who rejected God's prophets, Stephen was a living example of a prophet who received God's Word and responded to the Holy Spirit; the result was a powerful witness.

However, this witness only increased the religious leader's anger.

The Holy Spirit Reassures

Stephen was filled with the Holy Spirit when he looked up towards heaven and "saw the glory of God, and Jesus standing on the right hand of God" (Acts 7:55 KJV). Though Stephen saw Jesus *standing* at the right hand of God, but Jesus is *seated* in terms of His redemptive work, which was forever completed in His work on the cross. The writer of Hebrews said, "But this man, after he had offered one sacrifice for sins for ever, sat down on the right hand of God" (Hebrews 10:12 KJV).

Jesus was standing, showing His concern for Stephen—ready to welcome him into heaven. Stephen said, "I see the heavens opened, and the Son of man standing on the right hand of God" (Acts 7:56 KJV). The religious leaders had enough; their minds were made up, dulled to the Word of God. Stephen's vision and words describing who he saw, the King on the throne, solidified their hard-heartedness.

Those in the crowd covered their ears and rushed Stephen to drown out his voice with shouts (Acts 7:57). They drug him out and stoned him (Acts 7:58). Witnesses took off their coats and laid them at a young man's feet who was watching named Saul.

Stephen wasn't swayed, even as the stones pounded him. He prayed, "Lord Jesus, receive my spirit" (Acts 7:59 KJV). Falling to his knees he shouted, "lay not this sin to their charge" (Acts 7:60 KJV). Drawing his last breath, Stephen died and became the first martyr—a witness to Christ, to death. The Spirit of God never left him—He was with Stephen reassuring Him of God's presence while he was being stoned and as crossed from this world to the next.

The movement of the church explodes when believers are committed to the death like Stephen. Historically, the church has grown the most during times of darkest persecution. However, it takes bold faith and believers who are willing to speak the truth of God's Word, trusting Him for the increase, regardless of the consequences. Only then does God multiply His church like He did in those early days after Christ's resurrection.

The Holy Spirit Sets the Stage for Production Through Persecution

The Holy Spirit moved even more powerfully and productively after Stephen's death. His death marked a turning point in the history of the church. This is true of many periods of intense persecution.

For example, though Christians are undergoing some of the worst persecution in history in the Middle East, there is a surprising surge in the growth of Christianity. The Christian population is increasing; between Saudi Arabia and the United Arab Emirates, there are now well over one million Christians.[26]

The saints of the first century church had made a decision through the empowerment of the Holy Spirit to continue to speak boldly about Jesus, and this increased the momentum of the church movement. The Jews thought they had contained this nonsensical talk of Jesus but Stephen's death became an incentive to spread the gospel more. Though it seems backwards, the Holy Spirit sets the stage for church growth often through periods of terrible persecution.

There were about two thousand Christians martyred during these early years of the church. But the Holy Spirit empowered the saints to continue to make bold decisions for Christ and speak His gospel.

The Holy Spirit even set the stage for Paul's ministry by placing him in the midst of the Stephen's stoning! He was a young man at the time, with a goal to wipe out Jesus followers—which continued long after he witnessed Stephen's death (Acts 8:3). Stephen's stoning and Paul's own involvement in the persecution of the church impacted his later ministry, which was productive and fruitful. Likely those years of personally persecuting the church were what compelled him to make it known to the world who it was he had been persecuting.

What may have appeared as an unqualified tragedy was also, in fact, the Holy Spirit setting the stage for production, or multiplication, through persecution. It was the blood of Jesus, then the blood of Stephen and the martyrs that came behind Him, that watered the seeds of the gospel.

Christians are not immune to persecution today; though there may appear to be a season of calm, persecution will come in one way or another. It may be small, like isolation, but Christians must also be prepared for the possibility of persecution not unlike that of

Stephen. But take heart! God works all things—even persecution—for the good of those who love him, who have been called according to His purpose (Romans 8:28).

CHAPTER EIGHT

Facilitating the Spread of the Gospel

Acts 8

And the angel of the Lord spake unto Philip, saying, Arise, and go toward the south unto the way that goeth down from Jerusalem unto Gaza, which is desert. And he arose and went: and, behold, a man of Ethiopia, an eunuch of great authority under Candace queen of the Ethiopians, who had the charge of all her treasure, and had come to Jerusalem for to worship, Was returning, and sitting in his chariot read Esaias the prophet. Then the Spirit said unto Philip, Go near, and join thyself to this chariot. And Philip ran thither to him, and heard him read the prophet Esaias, and said, Understandest thou what thou readest? — Acts 8:26–30 (KJV)

Christianity did not stay in Jerusalem and the surrounding areas. Because of the boldness of the apostles who trusted in the power of the Holy Spirit, they carried the message of salvation beyond where they could have imagined or planned on their own. Obedience to the voice of the Spirit extended the opportunity for the gospel message to move out to the uttermost parts of the world. And it because of the persecution of the saints who who had begun to scatter throughout Judaea and Samaria to escape persecution that this spread of the gospel occurred. The movement of the church picked up speed.

But often, as new disciples joined the evangelism efforts, correction for skewed theology was necessary. Sometimes, the saints needed simple clarification, or education on certain truths.

The Scattering of the Saints

Stephen's death sparked a great persecution against the church that scattered the saints. Many new converts began to disperse throughout the region of Judaea and Samaria escaping persecution (with the exception of the apostles). The main reason followers of Jesus scattered was because of a certain man named Saul.

And at that time there was a great persecution against the church which was at Jerusalem; and they were all scattered abroad throughout the regions of Judaea and Samaria, except the apostles. And devout men carried Stephen to his burial, and made great lamentation over him. As for Saul, he made havock of the church, entering into every house, and haling men and women committed them to prison. — *Acts 8:1–3 (KJV)*

Saul went on a "seize the saints" mission to create havoc for the church in Acts 8:3. He tried his best to destroy, devastate and demolish the church. He entered Christians' homes, arrested them, and hauled them off to prison. Saul (also known as Paul) said himself that some Christians were put to death (Acts 26:10).

However, "they that were scattered abroad went every where preaching the word" (Acts 8:4 KJV). Satan's strategy was to destroy the church through its scattering but that was exactly what the church needed for it to spread.

To the Ends of the Earth

Philip, one of the twelve apostles and one of the deacons ordained in Acts 6, went to the Samaritans to spread the gospel. Recall that had been through that region before (John 4).

The word 'gentile' refers to anyone who is not Jewish. The Samaritans formed a link between the Jews and the gentiles, for they were a mongrel people, made up of both sorts, and holding both Jewish and pagan rites. In Matthew 10:5 Jesus told the twelve disciples *not* to go to the Samaritans. But when Philip preached, the Samaritans received him and great miracles occurred. Acts 8:12 says, "But when they believed Philip preaching the things concerning the kingdom of God, and the name of Jesus Christ, they were baptized, both men and women" (KJV). Great miracles and signs caused many to believe.

A Sorcerer's Salvation

Among those was a man named Simon, who after being baptized, continued with Philip to spread the gospel (Acts 8:12). Ancient records give a very strange depiction of Simon. It is said that he pretended to be the father that gave the law to Moses, that he came in the reign of Tiberius in the person of the Son; that he descended on the apostles on the day of Pentecost, in flames of fire, in quality of the Holy Spirit.[27] What is certain is that Simon used sorcery to bewitch the Samaritans (Acts 8:9), pretending to be somebody great. He confused their judgment by amazing them, coercing them to believe he had great powers of God. He fooled the Samaritans for a long time (Acts 8:9).

But when the Samaritans heard Philip preach they believed him. Simon's tricks were no match for the Savior's treasure. God's Word was what made the difference. Philip preached the Kingdom of God—that is, God's sovereign rule and the name of Jesus—"and the name of Jesus Christ, they were baptized, both men and women" (Acts 8:12 KJV). Simon believed as well and continued on with Philip (Acts 8:13).

A Strategic Movement and a Special Sign

When the apostles heard about how Samaritans were coming to faith, they sent Peter and John to pray and laid their hands on them that they might receive the Holy Ghost (Acts 8:15, 17). As holy as the deacons were, they were still under apostolic authority. Peter and John came to Samaria, "for as yet he was fallen upon none of them" (Acts 8:16 KJV); they had only been baptized in the name of the Lord Jesus. When the apostles laid they their hands on the new believers, they received the Holy Ghost (Acts 8:17). This was a strategic movement of the Spirit that no human being could have planned! The gospel had spread to the Samaritans, a group of people the Jews considered outcasts and avoided.

Why did the Samaritans have to wait for the apostles before the Holy Spirit came upon them? There are some who teach that believers receive the Holy Spirit *after* salvation, but they ignore the transitional nature of Acts. Romans 8:9 says, "But ye are not in the flesh, but in the Spirit, if so be that the Spirit of God dwell in you. Now if any man have not the Spirit of Christ, he is none of his" (KJV). There is no such thing as a Christian that does not yet have the Holy Spirit. Paul affirmed this in 1 Corinthians 12:13 when he said, "For by one Spirit are we all baptized into one body, whether we be Jews or Gentiles, whether we be bond or free; and have been all made to drink into one Spirit" (KJV).

Most scholars agree that God chose to pour out his Spirit after the apostles went to the Samaritans as a special sign for a few reasons.

It Marked a Moment in History

The spread of the gospel to Samaria was a strategic moment in the movement of the church. Because of the long history of conflict between Jews, Samaritans, and gentiles, this event was monumental and as such marked a specific moment in biblical history.

It Was a Crucial Moment for the New Church

The gospel had now spread beyond the Jews. It seemed as though God gave them their own Samaritan Pentecost, as He appeared to give Cornelius and his family an outpouring as well in Acts 10 as a sign of gentile conversion. To this point, the Holy Spirit entered a person's life at conversion; He baptized, sealed, and indwelled the person the moment they believed. This, however, was a special event.

It Was to Confirm and Incorporate

Peter and John came to the new believers to confirm them and incorporate them into the church. Philip was a deacon and it would take apostolic confirmation to confirm this transition in the formation of the church. This was a singled-out event that would not occur again. Peter and John gave credibility to the Samaritan spiritual movement.

If the Samaritans had received the Spirit without the apostles they would have never have come together with the Jewish believers. The rift would have remained and there could have very well been two churches when God's design is for one church.

The Holy Spirit expanded the stage to spread the gospel by scattering the saints and spreading salvation through unexpected evangelists like Simon, and to unexpected enemies like the Samaritans.

In retrospect, the strategy was divinely perfect. God had promised throughout Scripture that one day "all the ends of the earth will remember and turn to the LORD, and all the families of the nations will bow down before him" (Psalm 22:27 NIV). Salvation has never been solely for the Jews; Israel would be a light to the gentiles "that my salvation may reach to the ends of the earth" (Isaiah 49:6 NIV). In Acts 8, the mystery of how this would happen begins to be revealed.

The Holy Spirit Expands the Stage to Spread the Gospel Correction and Conversion

As the church continued to grow, the apostles were quick to rectify incorrect theology among its members. Simon was amazed by the Power of the Holy Spirit and wanted to purchase the power, offering them money for the ability to save people (Acts 8:18). Peter quickly intervened and corrected him, teaching Simon that the Spirit cannot be bought and censured Simon on the negativity of his heart. Sometimes, correction is necessary when a member of the church believes a skewed theology.

Simon responded, "Pray ye to the LORD for me, that none of these things which ye have spoken come upon me" (Acts 8:24 KJV). The apostles preached the Word and went on their way.

Clarification and Education

Next the angel of the Lord directed Philip, "Arise, and go toward the south unto the way that goeth down from Jerusalem unto Gaza, which is desert" (Acts 8:26 KJV). That road led him to an Ethiopian eunuch that had been traveling from Jerusalem back to Ethiopia. He was a government official in charge of the finances of Candace, the Queen of Ethiopia. The Holy Spirit led Philip to draw near and join him in his chariot.

The man was looking at the book of Isaiah. Philip heard him reading, jumped into the chariot and asked him, "Understandest thou what thou readest?" (Acts 8:30 KJV). The eunich's answer was, "How can I, except some man should guide me?" and he invited Philip to come and sit with him (Acts 8:31).

This eunich desired to be taught. Before Philip had even arrived, the eunich was reading Isaiah 53:7 which says, "He is [was] brought as a lamb to the slaughter, and as a sheep before her shearers is dumb, so he openeth not his mouth" (KJV). The eunuch asked Philip to tell him who Isaiah was speaking about. The Holy Spirit orchestrated for the two men to meet, but had already prepared the eunich's heart for what he was about to receive. Act 8:35 says, "Philip opened his mouth, and began at the same scripture, and preached unto him Jesus" (KJV).

The eunich only needed clarification and education on what he was reading. Sometimes followers of Jesus will need to come alongside people like the eunich and help them see what is right under their noses.

Opportunity, Observation, and Obedience

Philip seized the *opportunity* to preach Jesus. As the two men went on their way the eunuch made an observation. He *observed* a stream of water and said to Philip, "Here is water; what doth hinder me to be baptized?" to which Philip replied, "If thou believest with all thine heart, thou mayest" (Acts 8:36-37 KJV). Immediately the eunuch answered that he believed Jesus Christ is the Son of God (Acts 8:37).

Philip stopped at the chariot in *obedience* to the mandate Jesus left his disciples just before He ascended into heaven:

> *Go ye therefore, and teach all nations, baptizing them in the name of the Father, and of the Son, and of the Holy Ghost.* — *Matthew 28:19 (KJV)*

Both men stepped down into the water, and Philip baptized the eunich. Afterwards, "the Spirit of the Lord caught away Philip" and the eunich never saw him again (Acts 8:39 KJV). Twice Scripture highlights Philip's obedience.

Philip did not let the opportunity to minister to the eunuch slip by him, observed the situation, and followed the Holy Spirit's leading for what to do. The result was a new member in God's Kingdom, and the church movement continued.

The Spirit Empowers Believers to Correct

Acts 8 illustrates some of the functions of the Holy Spirit. Simon was symbolic of people in the early church and some present in church today—people who are fascinated with the power of the Holy Spirit but have not submitted to His power. Simon looked at the Spirit as entertainment. Becoming a Christian does not instantly resolve all problems and character flaws. New believers must be nurtured in the faith.

Some people debate whether Simon was really saved or not, but this was not the real issue; he needed correction and re-direction. His that was centered on excitement with no lifestyle change. The Holy Spirit is not a tool for making money!

The Spirit Engages Believers to Do the Work of Ministry

Philip was engaged to do the work, a characteristic modern day followers of Jesus do not often exhibit. Consider again Jesus' words in Matthew 28:

> Go ye therefore, and teach all nations, baptizing them in the name of the Father, and of the Son, and of the Holy Ghost: Teaching them to observe all things whatsoever I have commanded you: and, lo, I am with you always, even unto the end of the world. Amen. — *Matthew 28:19–20 (KJV)*

Jesus' first directive in His Great Commission was, "Go ye therefore" (Matthew 28:19 KJV). Philip understood this, and stepped out in faith as the Holy Spirit instructed him. But believers are today are empowered by the Holy Spirit to witness just as Philip was.

The Spirit also engages believers to teach others about Jesus Christ. The eunuch obviously had some knowledge of God but not of Jesus Christ. Philip observed the "Teaching them to observe all things whatsoever I have commanded you" (Matthew 28:20 KJV) part of the Great Commission, taught the eunuch about Jesus Christ, and immediately baptized him.

Philip was obedient to the voice of the Holy Spirit and was engaged to do the work. He was bold and not afraid to open his mouth—even if persecuted. The basis of Philip's message was the Word of God. The Bible says Philip "Began at the same scripture" the eunich was currently puzzled about (Acts 8:35) ... and the eunich was saved.

The Holy Spirit empowered Philip's witness to be the beginning of the witness to the ends of the earth. Ethiopia was in Africa. The Jews had contact with Ethiopia in ancient days according to Psalms 68:31 and Jeremiah 38:7. The eunuch may have become a gentile convert to Judaism but because of his conversion to Christ, Christianity spread to another part of the world. Obedience to the voice of the Spirit extends the opportunity for the gospel message to the uttermost parts of the world.

CHAPTER NINE

Changing Perspectives

Acts 9

And straightway he preached Christ in the synagogues, that he is the Son of God. — Acts 9:20 (KJV)

The movement of the church was something the known world had never experienced—and the disciples' message was peculiar. A God-man crucified, died, and resurrected? The role of the Holy Spirit manifested powerful in those early years, through signs and wonders to validate these claims. However, these miracles were not for show; they had a specific purpose. Two types of miracles occurred in this chapter of Acts: one transformed a person's heart, and the other healed the sick and brought the dead back to life. Though both were validated with witnesses, some types of signs and wonders did not continue to the present day.

The Holy Spirit Sanctifies

Up to this point in Acts, first-century believers were only converted when someone shared the gospel with them. The Holy Spirit then began the work of sanctification in that person's life. Sanctification means "to make holy," in the sense that God is holy[28]—as Isaiah declared: "And one cried unto another, and said, Holy, holy, holy, is the LORD of hosts: the whole earth is full of his glory" (Isaiah 6:3 KJV). Paul said in 2 Corinthians 5:17 says, "Therefore if any man be in Christ, he is a new creature: old things are passed away; behold, all things are become new" (KJV). Sanctification is the progression of becoming a "new creature" as a result of the indwelling of the Holy Spirit.

Then in Acts 9, one of the biggest opponents of the church—Saul—experienced a miraculous conversion, resulting in a complete transformation of character and purpose. Saul become one of the leading advocates for the church. Saul's conversion is one of the strongest arguments for the resurrection of Jesus Christ and evidence of the transforming power of the the Holy Spirit.

Persecution and Perspective

To Saul, the movement of Christianity was cultic went against everything he was taught as a devout Jew. By his own account, Saul wanted nothing to do with Jesus Christ and was at his peak in his goals to persecute the church. He had such disdain for Christians that he went to the high priest and asked for consent to go to Damascus into the synagogues to arrest Christians and bring them in bonds to Jerusalem. Christians were known as people of "the way," which has its probable origin in two statements of Jesus; Matthew 7:13–14 and John 14:6.

Enter ye in at the strait gate: for wide is the gate, and broad is the way, that leadeth to destruction, and many there be which go in thereat: Because strait is the gate, and narrow is the way, which leadeth unto life, and few there be that find it. — **Matthew 7:13–14 (KJV)**

Jesus saith unto him, I am the way, the truth, and the life: no man cometh unto the Father, but by me. — **John 14:6 (KJV)**

As Saul journeyed near Damascus a light shone from heaven and He fell to the earth. Saul heard a voice saying, "Saul, Saul, why persecutes thou me? (Acts 9:4). Saul asked, "Who art thou Lord?" and Jesus responded by saying, "I am Jesus whom thou persecutes: it is hard for thee to kick against the pricks" (Acts 9:5 KJV). God told Saul he was hurting no one but himself. Trembling and astonished Saul said, "Lord, what wilt thou have me to do?" (Acts 9:6 KJV).

Saul experienced a divine change in perspective that day. He went from opposing Jesus to becoming obedient to Jesus. Jesus instructed Saul to go into the city where he would receive instructions for what to do next (Acts 9:6). The men that were with him stood speechless because they heard the voice but could not see anyone (Acts 9:7). Rising from the ground, Saul found he was blind and had to be led into the city by the men. He remained blind for three days and nights "and neither did eat nor drink" (Acts 9:9 KJV).

Persecuting Christians had been Saul's life's mission until he encountered Jesus when his world was turned upside down.

As Saul was experiencing this major life change, God was also speaking to a disciple living in Damascus named Ananias through a vision. Ananias was instructed to get up and go down to a street called Straight (Acts 9:11) and enter the home of a man named Judas where he would find Saul of Tarsus praying. God told Ananias He had prepared Saul for Ananias's visit; Saul had already seen Ananias in a vision coming to lay hands on him that his sight might be restored.

Ananias said, "Lord, I have heard by many of this man, how much evil he hath done to thy saints at Jerusalem" (Acts 9:13 KJV). He knew Saul was an enemy of God, and thus his enemy too! Could God be wrong? But the Lord told Ananias that Saul was "a chosen vessel unto me, to bear my name before the Gentiles, and kings, and the children of Israel: For I will shew him how great things he must suffer for my name's sake" (Acts 9:15–16 KJV).

Ananias obeyed, went to Saul and laid hands on him. Saul was filled with the Holy Ghost, received his sight, got up and was baptized. Saul began to eat and regain strength, as he remained several more days with the Saints in Damascus. The saints could not believe that this was the same man who a few days earlier was on a mission to murder Christians. Saul, with a changed perspective and a new determination, set out on a mission to prove that Jesus is the resurrected Christ.

The Holy Spirit Can Change Anyone

The Holy Spirit confirms the resurrection of Christ through Jesus' worst critics; if He can transform Paul, He can change anyone.

Later Paul (Saul's Greek name) acknowledged this transformation and was able to say, "For I am the least of the apostles, that am not meet to be called an apostle, because I persecuted the church of God" (1 Corinthians 15:9 KJV). Only the power of the Holy Spirit can transform a person like Saul; God changed his mission to be focused on loving the people he had spent years trying to persecute (and even kill). So, too, can the Spirit work miracles in the lives others in your life—even those who are the most antagonistic toward Christ.

Church Resilience in Spite of Rising Conflict

Rising conflict ensued as Saul become one of the leading voices in the community preaching about Jesus Christ. The Jews were livid. Saul went from killing Christians for the Jewish community, to being sought after by the Jews who wanted him dead.

The Jews waited day and night to catch Saul but there were people who helped him escape. He immediately tried to set up a rendezvous in Jerusalem with the disciples but they were afraid of him and were not convinced of his conversion. Barnabas, the encourager from the end Acts 4, declared to the disciples how Saul "had seen the Lord in the way, and that he had spoken to him, and how he had preached boldly at Damascus in the name of Jesus" (Acts 9:27 KJV). After Barnabas's testimony, the disciples believed and accepted Saul.

Saul began to go in and out of Jerusalem with the disciples preaching uninhibitedly about Jesus Christ. He encountered opposition with a group of Greek-speaking Jews called Hellenists who plotted to murder him. However, his friends helped him escape to a town called Caesarea, and shipped him off to Tarsus.

The church experienced a period of rest for a time (Acts 9:31). All over the country— Judea, Samaria, and in the Galilee—the church grew. Its people experienced a deep sense of reverence for God and knew the Holy Spirit was with them and was strengthening them.

The church displayed resilience in the face of opposition, propelling the movement to out from Jerusalem.

The Holy Spirit Counters Opposition and Compels the Saints

Though the Jews opposed Saul, the Holy Spirit countered their opposition with increased church grown. This encouraged and engaged the saints to move forward even more.

Circling back to Acts 9:31 Luke wrote that as the church grew, its members "were edified" and they walked "in the fear of the Lord, and in the comfort of the Holy Ghost." To be 'edified' is the Greek word *oikodomeō*, which means "to build a house, to erect a building up from the foundation." It can also mean "to restore by building or rebuild or repair."[29]

First Peter 2:5 says that God's people, like living stones, "are being built into a spiritual house to be a holy priesthood, offering spiritual sacrifices acceptable to God through Jesus Christ" (NIV). In spite of opposition, God continued to build His house "up from the foundation."

The Holy Spirit Worked Miracles

Sometime later, Peter came to Lydda—a town near Joppa on the Mediterranean. There he healed a man named Aeneas, and all who witnessed the miracle turned to the Lord (Acts 9:35). In Joppa Peter also healed a woman named Tabitha. Tabitha had died, and had already been prepared for burial (Acts 9:37). Peter knelt down beside the dead body and prayed, commanding Tabitha to rise. Acts 9:40 says, "She opened her eyes, and seeing Peter she sat up" (NIV). The news spread throughout Joppa and many people believed (Acts 9:42).

Clearly the Holy Spirit played a powerful role in the expansion of the early church. Filled with the Spirit, Peter was empowered do the work of evangelism through miracles. The early church prayed for God to show signs and wonders (Acts 4:29–30) and God granted those requests. Sick people were healed by Peter's shadow and possessed people made well (Acts 5:12–16). Stephen healed performed great wonders and signs (Acts

6:8). Philip proclaimed the message of Jesus in Samaria, followed by signs and wonders; impure spirits came out of people and lame people were healed and baptized (Acts 8:4–8, 12–13). Saul heard the gospel from Christ himself and then received a sign—Ananais placed his hands on Saul's blind eyes and "immediately there fell from his eyes as it had been scales: and he received sight forthwith, and arose, and was baptized" (Acts 9:18 KJV). Signs, wonders and miracles in the early church awakened and encouraged faith in the gospel being preached.

Evidence of Miracles Today?

There is no biblical evidence that believers can perform miracles like the early church. Some use Mark 16:17–18 to argue the opposite: "And these signs shall follow them that believe; In my name shall they cast out devils; they shall speak with new tongues; They shall take up serpents; and if they drink any deadly thing, it shall not hurt them; they shall lay hands on the sick, and they shall recover" (KJV). They see this to mean that Christ was speaking to *every* believer when in fact he was speaking directly to the eleven disciples and commissioning them to preach the gospel.

Afterwards the disciples went out, preached, and performed miracles. Jesus confirmed their preaching through signs. The Word was preached first and the signs and wonders followed to validate the new leaders of the church. This is why Paul was able to say, "Truly the signs of an apostle were wrought among you in all patience, in signs, and wonders, and mighty deeds" (2 Corinthians 12:12 KJV) and, "Through mighty signs and wonders, by the power of the Spirit of God; so that from Jerusalem, and round about unto Illyricum, I have fully preached the gospel of Christ" (Romans 15:19 KJV).

Spiritual transformation occurs every day as people put their faith in Christ and are brought from death to life. However, the kinds of miracles, signs and wonders evident in the early church do not occur. In first century Christianity, their purpose was to reveal God's will and establish the foundation of the church. God can do whatever He chooses and if He decides to do a miracle today, His will be done. However, the Bible is now complete and readily accessible—something first century believers did not have. They preached the Word verbally, and signs and wonders followed as confirmation. Disciples of Christ must instead commit to study His Word where God will reveal truth, as opposed to looking for signs and wonders to convert the lost.

CHAPTER TEN

Penetrating Prejudices

Acts 10

To him give all the prophets witness, that through his name whosoever believeth in him shall receive remission of sins. While Peter yet spake these words, the Holy Ghost fell on all them which heard the word. And they of the circumcision which believed were astonished, as many as came with Peter, because that on the Gentiles also was poured out the gift of the Holy Ghost. — Acts 10:43-45 (KJV)

God does not prefer some people groups over others, or one person over someone else. God loves *all* people and desires that all come to a saving faith. Scripture says, "For God so loved the world, that he gave his only begotten Son, that whosoever believeth in him should not perish, but have everlasting life" in (John 3:16 KJV). He didn't say some, or even those who were good. He loves all people.

However, people are people. They are by nature sinful, and struggle with insecurities and pride. When personal hang-ups or unrecognized prejudices are mixed with evangelism attempts it can hinder the gospel. This is what happened in the early church, and God was quick to intervene and set the apostles straight; His intention was the gospel go out to the entire world, not just to the Jews.

A Gospel for the Gentiles

There were many cultural differences between Jews and gentiles that confined the apostles' ministry to Jews and circumcised proselytes. Until this point, there had been no attempt to offer Christ to gentiles because Jews believed no one could be saved and go to heaven unless they were fully obedient to the law of Moses and circumcised. The issue of circumcision prevented the apostles from preaching to those who were not circumcised.

The only way these prejudices could be reversed was through the power of the Holy Spirit. The apostles and the new Jewish converts needed to be convinced God had extended salvation to *everyone* and not just the Jews

The Command to Cornelius

In Acts 10:1–8, God sent a vision to a centurion named Cornelius. A centurion was a chief or captain of one hundred men. Cornelius was over the Italian regiment (band) and he and his family worshipped the true God. He gave much alms. His love for God led him to love men; this love proved its sincerity by his actions. He was a praying man.

It was the ninth hour of the day when God allowed him to see a vision of the angel of God coming to him, calling his name. He responded by saying, "What is it Lord?" (Acts 10:4 KJV). The angel said, "Thy prayers and thine alms are come up for a memorial before God" (Acts 10:4 KJV). A "memorial before God" reminded God of those who were worshippers like Cornelius who needed God's protection and help (Leviticus 2:16).

God commanded Cornelius to send men to Joppa to get Simon, "whose surname is Peter: He lodgeth with one Simon a tanner, whose house is by the sea side: he shall tell thee what thou oughtest to do" (Acts 10:5–6 KJV). Everyone called this man "Peter," and he was staying with another man named Simon—a Tanner.

After the angel left, Cornelius called two servants and one particularly devout soldier from the guard. He explained to them everything that happened and sent them off to Joppa.

The Priming of Peter

God had already primed Peter for breaking down old barriers and beliefs. The next day, while the three men journeyed to fetch him, Peter went up to the roof to pray and grew hungry. While lunch was being prepared, he fell into a trance and saw the sky open. He saw what looked a huge blanket lowered by ropes at its four corners settled on the ground with every imaginable animal on it. And he heard Jesus say, "Rise, Peter; kill, and eat." Peter's response reflected a typical Jewish understanding: "Not so, Lord; for I have never eaten any thing that is common or unclean." Peter was taken aback; He knew from the law he was not supposed to eat food that was "unclean," or food that was not kosher.

A second time the voice said, "What God hath cleansed, that call not thou common." After the voice spoke a third time, the blanket was pulled back up into the sky leaving Peter to ponder what the vision meant. The three men showed up at Peter's front door and asked for him—but Peter was lost in thought. The Holy Spirit whispered to him that three men were knocking at the door looking for him (Acts 10:19). "Arise therefore, and get thee down, and go with them, doubting nothing: for I have sent them," the Spirit said (Acts 10:20 KJV).

Peter went down to the men and let them know they had found whom they were looking for (Acts 10:21). The three men responded, "Cornelius the centurion, a just man, and one that feareth God, and of good report among all the nation of the Jews, was warned from God by an holy angel to send for thee into his house, and to hear words *of thee.*"

Peter invited them into Simon (the Tanner's) house and the three men stayed the night.

The Clarity of the Conference

It was then Peter discovered why Cornelius had sent for him. The next day when Peter reached Cornelius, his relatives and friends were waiting for him. When Peter

came through the door, Cornelius greeted him then fell
down worshiping him (Acts 10:25). Peter pulled him up
and reprimanded him, saying:

> *Stand up; I myself also am a man. And as he talked with*
> *him, he went in, and found many that were come together.*
> *And he said unto them, Ye know how that it is an unlawful*
> *thing for a man that is a Jew to keep company, or come*
> *unto one of another nation; but God hath shewed me that I*
> *should not call any man common or unclean. Therefore*
> *came I unto you without gainsaying, as soon as I was sent*
> *for: I ask therefore for what intent ye have sent for me? —*
> ***Acts 10:26–29 (KJV)***

Peter made it clear that he was no different from
anyone present and that eating separately from gentiles
was only a Jewish custom (by tradition, Jews were not
supposed to eat with others of another race).

Peter shared his vision with the men, telling them God
had showed him he should not call *any* man clean or
unclean (Acts 10:28). Cornelius responded by sharing
with Peter what had happened to him—that four days
prior as he was praying a man appeared and told his
prayers and neighborly acts had brought God's attention,
and that he was to send to get Peter from the Tanner's
house. "Now therefore are we all here present before
God, to hear all things that are commanded thee of God,"
Cornelius declared (Acts 10:33 KJV)

The Gospel Message Destroys Prejudices

Cornelius gave Peter permission to preach, and Peter didn't miss the opportunity. Peter said he now understood that God was no respecter of persons and if someone desired a relationship with God and was ready to do what He said, the door was wide open. The good news of Jesus Christ was for all; anyone could be saved.

Peter began to preach the story of Jesus Christ arriving from Nazareth, anointed by God with the Holy Spirit, helping people and healing everyone who was beaten down by the devil. He explained that because of Jesus' works, He was hung on a cross, killed and buried but in three days God raised Him from the dead. "We are witnesses of all things which he did both in the land of the Jews, and in Jerusalem; whom they slew and hanged on a tree," Peter proclaimed (Acts 10:39 KJV).

Peter explained how Jesus handpicked him and others and how they ate and drank with him after He came back from the dead. He told the men how Jesus commissioned them to preach everywhere they went that Jesus was the One whom God destined as Judge of the living and dead and how He is the means to forgiveness of sins, "that through his name whosoever believeth in him shall receive remission of sins" (Acts 10:43 KJV).

Then, all at once, the Holy Spirit came upon the listeners and the Jews who came with Peter witnessed the gift of the Holy Spirit being poured out on "outsiders." Gentiles received the Holy Spirit. The Jews were astonished as they heard gentiles speaking in tongues and praising God.

Peter asked if anyone present would reject to baptizing those gentiles with water—since they had "received the Holy Ghost as well as we" (Acts 10:47 KJV). And so, the first gentiles were baptized in the name of Jesus Christ. Later, Paul would pen a letter to the Galatian church in which he said, "There is no longer Jew or Gentile, slave or free, male and female. For you are all one in Christ Jesus" (Galatians 3:28 NLT). All people regardless of cultural, ethnic or even religious background—when they believe in Jesus—are baptized into one body, "whether Jew or Greeks, slave or free" (1 Corinthians 12:13 BSB).

God does not play favorites. He longs for all people to know Him and be known by Him (Galatians 2:9). For the church movement to continue and reach the world in the power of the Spirit like it did in the first century, racial, ethnic and cultural prejudices must be cast aside. When believers commit to follow God's instruction, obedient to Him and His Word, the Holy Spirit goes ahead to prepare people's hearts in order to break through prejudices and cultural practices. And the gospel goes out.

CHAPTER ELEVEN

Changing Attitudes

Acts 11

When they heard these things, they held their peace, and glorified God, saying, Then hath God also to the Gentiles granted repentance unto life. — *Acts 11:18 (KJV)*

Change is not easy especially when traditions are involved. In Acts 10, the Holy Spirit had penetrated the prejudicial cultural practices of staunch Jewish Christians who learned God is no respecter of persons. It was tough to accept and embrace, at first, but the result was the inclusion of gentile believers in God's church.

Now, in Acts 11, the Holy Spirit was creating change in the church that would require breaking from old traditions—and there were many that took offense. It was uncomfortable, and different. However, attitudes needed to change if the church was going to continue to expand. When change is at hand there more often than not are folks who will come against the change—and might need an attitude adjustment so a great movement within the church can occur.

The Critics Are Convinced of the Change

The news of the gentiles' conversion and receiving of Holy Ghost spread quickly along with the rumors that Peter had eaten with gentiles. Peter's associates reprimanded him for eating and socializing with gentiles for it was against Jewish tradition (Acts 11:3). Peter was ruining the reputation of good Jews (Acts 11:3). He began to tell his story in detail from the beginning (Acts 11:4), including the vision he had from Acts 10. He explained how he had come to the understanding that the vision was not just about him eating traditionally clean or unclean foods but how God made everyone clean that had accepted Him. He further expressed why it was important for the Jews to change their attitudes about how they viewed the gentiles.

Peter explained how the Holy Spirit fell on the gentiles the same way it fell upon them (Acts 11:15) and how he had remembered the words of Jesus Christ: "For John truly baptized with water; but ye shall be baptized with the Holy Ghost not many days hence" (Acts 1:5 KJV).

Peter then asked, "Forasmuch then as God gave them the like gift as he did unto us, who believed on the Lord Jesus Christ; what was I, that I could withstand God?" (Acts 11:17 KJV). How could Peter object to what God was doing?

When the Jews heard Peter's account, they first became quiet. But then, the Message Version says when Peter's words "sank in, they started praising God" (Acts 11:18 MSG). They realized God had broken down cultural barriers and opened up salvation to everyone. The Jewish believers' attitudes were turned upside down!

The Climate of Attitudinal Change

After Stephen's persecution, the church was scattered mainly because of Saul's (and others') tirade. Saul was aggressively seeking to imprison and kill Christians. The scattered believers traveled to Phoenicia, Cyprus and Antioch preaching to Jews first but they eventually started preaching to the gentiles (Acts 11:19). Some of the believers were from Cyprus and Cyrene so they went to Antioch to preach Jesus to the Greeks (Acts 11:19). The hand of the Lord was with them and a great number believed, and turned unto the Lord (Acts 11:21).

As the gospel went forth, the church's whole attitudinal climate changed. When the church in Jerusalem found out what was happening they sent Barnabas to Antioch find out if it was of God (Acts 11:22). When Barnabas arrived he saw that God was indeed at work. He affirmed the disciples' work and urged and encouraged them to press on; the church in Antioch grew strong (Acts 11:23–24).

Barnabas found Saul who was in Tarsus, and together they preached and taught in Antioch for "a whole year" (Acts 11:26 MSG). "It was in Antioch that the disciples were for the first time called Christians (Acts 11:26 MSG).

Though at first resistant to change, once the people realized the magnitude of what the Holy Spirit was doing—the inclusion of the gentiles in God's church—they rejoiced and embraced their new God-given vision.

The Confirmation of Change

Some prophets had come from Jerusalem to Antioch. One prophet named Agabus, stood up. Prompted by the Spirit, he warned a famine was coming that would devastate the country (Acts 11:28). Just as Agabus foretold, the famine occurred during the rule of Claudius Caesar (Acts 11:28).

The disciples decided to help and to "send relief unto the brethren which dwelt in Judaea" (Acts 11:29 KJV). They sent Barnabas and Saul "to deliver the collection to the leaders in Jerusalem" (Acts 11:29 MSG).

Though it might seem out of place at the end of the chapter, the Holy Spirit inspired Luke (its writer) to place this story here intentionally. It shows followers of Christ when they follow the movement of the Holy Spirit, effective ministry results. When believers help those in need, their love and care affirms the movement of the Spirit and validates the gospel.

Proper Alignment Produces Effective Change

It is paramount believers follow the direction of the Holy Spirit and not try to persuade the Holy Spirit to follow them. However, where the Holy Spirit leads won't always be comfortable. Sometimes when the Holy Spirit initiates changes within the church contention will arise among the people.

Change is especially difficult when traditions are involved. Sometimes those most resistant to change *appear* holy, as the Jews did, yet they will mask their contention in other ways without expressing what they are really upset about. But the Holy Spirit will cause change to occur in the church regardless of man's willingness to embrace it.

The church should always be ready to convince critics of change—knowing ultimately this is out of obedience to the One initiating the change. There are a number of ways believers can check their own and their church's attitude regarding change—about God's preacher, God's promises, and God's power.

Check Your Attitude about God's Preacher

The Jewish critics may not have liked what Peter said, but they respected him. He was the preacher God chose to communicate a message.

They allowed Peter to explain why he had accepted these gentiles as brothers and sisters in the faith. Paul spoke of the importance of embracing this kind of attitude when he quoted God's words to Moses from Exodus 33:19: "What shall we say then? Is there unrighteousness with God? God forbid. For he saith to Moses, I will have mercy on whom I will have mercy, and I will have compassion on whom I will have compassion" (Romans 9:14–15 KJV). God will do all He pleases (Isaiah 46:10).

So, too, must the church's attitude be today in order for the movement to continue. When confronted with change, believers should process information by seeing if it is consistent with God's Word before responding. Today's "Peter," or "preacher," who may be initiating change is a voice piece for the Holy Spirit. If it appears the issue at hand is a leading of the Spirit, the church should humbly accept the change and watch God work!

Check Your Attitude about God's Promises

Checking to see if the change is consistent with God's Word involves comparing the proposed change with God's promises. In Acts 11, what Peter was proclaiming aligned with both Jesus and Paul's words. Jesus had commanded His disciples in Matthew 28:19–20 to go and teach all nations, and in John 3:16 Jesus had declared salvation was anyone who believes.

The Jews could trust Peter's words regarding gentile inclusion because what he said did not come against what Jesus had already declared. Later, Paul would affirm these truths to the Romans when he said, "For there is no difference between the Jew and the Greek: for the same Lord over all is rich unto all that call upon him. For whosoever shall call upon the name of the Lord shall be saved" (Romans 10:12–13 KJV).

Check Your Attitude about God's Power

Finally, always remember the Holy Spirit is in control, not the church. The apostle John wrote, "The wind bloweth where it listeth, and thou hearest the sound thereof, but canst not tell whence it cometh, and whither it goeth: so is every one that is born of the Spirit" (John 3:8 KJV).

Jesus used two words in reference to the activity of the Holy Ghost in John 3:8: 'wind' and 'spirit.' Though they are two words in English, in the Greek they are the same word: *pneuma*, which means "breath."[30] This is where the word 'pneumonia' comes from.

In the Bible, wind is symbollic of the Holy Spirit and by nature He is unpredictable and invisible—like the wind. He is totally free of man's control. Dutch Theologian Abraham Kuyper wrote of this invisibility of the Spirit: "The Holy Spirit leaves no footprints."[31] In other words, the Holy Spirit governs Himself and goes where He chooses.

So, too, must the church follow the Spirit and not try to convince the Spirit to follow it.

Change is inevitable, especially within the church. How God calls the church to operate in one generation (or even year!) may be different the next. When believers dig in their heels and resist change, they must consider they could be coming against the movement of the Holy Spirit—and preventing incredible growth.

You were asked to write out your 3-step plan for evangelism this week. Spend the remaining time discussing how your group will get the entire church involved in evangelism.

CHAPTER TWELVE

The Power of a Praying Church

Acts 12

Peter therefore was kept in prison: but prayer was made without ceasing of the church unto God for him. — *Acts 12:5 (KJV)*

The Holy Spirit was the agent of attitudinal change within the early church, challenging disciples to change traditional views, prejudices and opinions in Acts 11. In Acts 12, God's Word reveals that often the Holy Spirit allows circumstances both within the church and to the church to cause people pray.

When tragedy strikes, division occurs, persecution increases or false leadership rises, the Holy Spirit will assist the prayer life of the church. God's Spirit will exceed the expectations of the church that prays; the power of a praying church is often underestimated.

A Church in Persecution

King Herod Agrippa I had become a great enemy and chief persecutor of the church. Yet through His oppression the church discovered the awesome power of prayer as a spiritual weapon that prevails over persecution.

Herod created many problems for the fledgling church. He was the grandson of Herod the Great who ruled during the time of Jesus' birth (see Matthew 2:1–16). Herod discovered the more he persecuted the church the more his celebrity status with the Jews increased. He killed James (Son of Zebedee) with the sword, beheading him (Acts 12:2). This was a significant milestone in the history of the church. Whereas Stephen was a deacon and the first martyr to die, James was the first of the twelve apostles that followed Jesus to be martyred; he had been part of Jesus' inner circle along with his brother John, and Peter. It shattered the illusion that the apostles had protective immunity from persecution. This intense persecution should not have come as a surprise— Jesus warned the apostles to expect persecution, saying:

And the brother shall deliver up the brother to death, and the father the child: and the children shall rise up against their parents, and cause them to be put to death.

And ye shall be hated of all men for my name's sake: but he that endureth to the end shall be saved. — **Matthew 10:21–22 (KJV)**

Just as Jesus foretold, after Stephen's execution, a "great persecution broke out against the church in Jerusalem" (Acts 8:1 NIV).

Persecution Leads to Effective Prayer

Herod saw that putting James to death pleased the crowd, so during the days of unleavened bread (Passover week) he had Peter arrested and thrown into prison, intending to kill him after Passover (Acts 12:4). Herod placed Peter on maximum security under "four quaternions of soldiers "(Acts 12:5 KJV). A quaternion was four groups of guards with four guards each, totaling sixteen.

Acts 12:5 said that while Peter was "kept in prison…" (NIV) prayer was made without ceasing of the church unto God for him." The church prayed unto God on Peter's behalf. The prayers of the church produced powerful results and Peter was freed from prison by the angel of the Lord (Acts 12:7). "He thought he was seeing a vision" (Acts 12:9 NIV), but Scripture says he obeyed the angel and escaped passed the guards and through the city gate and went straight to Mary's house (Acts 12:7–12), John Mark's mother. There he found " many were gathered together praying."

It is interesting that the first apostle to be martyred was the same James who penned the words: "The effectual fervent prayer of a righteous man availeth much" (James 5:16 KJV).

While Peter was in chains, the church was praying for his release. And God heard.

The Saints in Disbelief

Peter went straightaway to Mary's house, John Mark's mother. This is John, the author of the Gospel by the same name. When Peter arrived at Mary's house, he knocked but he was not immediately let in. A young girl named Rhoda went to answer the door and when she heard Peter's voice she went to the prayer band and announced that "Peter stood before the gate" (Acts 12:14 KJV).

The disciples did not believe that it was Peter in the flesh and told Rhooda she had gone mad (Acts 12:15). Though she persisted, they concluded it was an angel (Acts 12:15).

It was a common opinion among the Jews of the time that every man had a guardian angel; they also believed that angels assumed the likeness of people. It is possible that the disciples at Mary's house thought Peter had been executed in prison and that his spirit showed up as a warning.

They finally let him in and began to celebrate his deliverance from prison. Peter immediately told them, "Go shew these things unto James, and to the brethren" (Acts 12:17 KJV).

The story is told of a small town in which there were no liquor stores. Eventually, a nightclub was built right on Main Street. Members of one of the churches in the area were so disturbed that they conducted several all-night prayer meetings, and asked the Lord to burn down that den of iniquity. Lightning struck the tavern a short time later, and it was completely destroyed by fire. The owner, knowing how the church people had prayed, sued them for the damages. His attorney claimed that their prayers had caused the loss. The congregation, on the other hand, hired a lawyer and fought the charges. After much deliberation the judge declared, "It's the opinion of this court that wherever the guilt may lie, the tavern keeper is the one who really believes in prayer while the church members do not."[32]

Though lighthearted, the point is paramount: prayer results in the miraculous and sometimes unexplainable furthering of the gospel.

The Soldiers in Dismay

At daybreak, the jail was in an uproar and the soldiers were in dismay looking for Peter (Acts 12:18). It was impossible for Peter to escape without human intervention! When Herod sent for him, and the soldiers could neither produce him nor explain where Peter was, Herod "ordered their execution" (Acts 12:19 MSG). Herod was angry; he adamantly wanted to kill Peter as he was the main figure in the Christian movement at that time. Scripture says, "He went down from Judaea to Caesarea" and dwelt there for a time (Acts 12:19 KJV).

The Sinners' Downfall

While in Caesarea, things went from bad to worse for Herod. He was at odds with the people of Tyre and Sidon. Scripture does not illuminate what the issue was, and no historians have related Herod's displeasure with

Tyre and Sidon. But the people of the cities recruited Blastus, probably a eunuch of Herod, to try and solve the problem. They needed Herod for food supplies. When they finally met to settle differences, Herod appeared arrogant as ever, took his place on the throne, and began to rattle off a lot of pompous jargon. The people began to flatter him saying, "It is the voice of God and not of a man" (Acts 12:22 KJV).

That was the last straw. The Message Version says, "God had had enough of Herod's arrogance and sent an angel to strike him down" (Acts 12:23 MSG). Herod had not given God credit for anything. In the words of the late Dr. Caesar Clark: "The worms got him!"[33] Down Herod went.

Fighting God Never Works

When people try and exalt themselves above God, it never works. Samuel, an Old Testament seer and prophet said:

> *If ye will fear the LORD, and serve him, and obey his voice, and not rebel against the commandment of the Lord, then shall both ye and also the king that reigneth over you continue following the LORD your God: But if ye will not obey the voice of the LORD, but rebel against the commandment of the LORD, then shall the hand of the LORD be against you, as it was against your fathers." — 1* **Samuel 12:14–15 (KJV)**

There are consequences for disobeying God and rebelling against His instruction; Scripture is clear God's hand will "be against you" (1 Samuel 12:15 KJV). Herod thought he could fight God and win. History is filled with stories of men who thought they could fight God and succeed; their ruined lives are evidence that it can't be done. Consider Friedrich Nietsche. Nietsche was a philosopher who coined the idea that God was dead, and that Christianity was a despised religion of "weaklings." He spent his life fighting God and sadly, became insane and spent the last years of his life mentally disturbed.[34]

As Herod's reign was deteriorating (likely a result of his rebellion against God) the ministry of God's Word grew by leaps and bounds. Acts 12:25 says that Barnabas and Saul "delivered the relief offering to the church in Jerusalem, went back to Antioch. This time they took John with them" (MSG), and the Word of God grew and multiplied.

Jesus warned persecution would come; who could expect the church to experience peace and safety when its leader was crucified? However, the Holy Spirit uses even the most horrible persecution to grow people in their faith—sometimes in supernatural, unexplainable ways. In Acts 12, Peter's persecution and imprisonment caused the church to rally together in prayer. Their faithful intercession before God resulted in Peter's miraculous release. The church strengthened in faith, and continued to grow.

When tragedy strikes, division occurs, persecution increases or false leadership rises, the Holy Spirit will assist the prayer life of the church. God's Spirit will exceed the expectations of the church that commits to trusting God through prayer.

CHAPTER THIRTEEN

Equipping Those God Calls

Acts 13

The Word of God changes lives, and God calls the church to deliver His Word by proclaiming it to a lost word.

Yet some people reject God's Word. How should the church respond to rejection? How is the church challenged by people who quit? Why do you think people quit in ministry?

And what is the difference between sinners and workers of iniquity? How should the church respond against workers of iniquity?

In the previous chapter, we read the account of how the Holy Spirit used the prayers of the church to free Peter from prison. In this chapter, we observe a shift in leadership from Peter to Paul. This chapter focuses primarily on Saul/Paul and Barnabas

134 · OSCAR T. MOSES

Inexperienced Experts

Antioch was a city blessed with many prophets and teachers. The Holy Spirit specifically assigned Paul (Saul's Greek name) and Barnabas particularly to preach the gospel to the gentiles. "Separate me Barnabas and Saul for the work whereunto I have called them," God said in Acts 13:2 (KJV). Their appointment came after church leadership prayed and fasted (Acts 13:3).

Paul and Barnabas set sail for Cyprus and preached in the synagogues to the Jews (Acts 13:5). John Mark assisted them. However, whenever the Holy Spirit is moving, the devil is close behind trying to disrupt God's plan from coming to pass—and often this comes in the form of opposition. Opposition was a primary theme of the early church.

Paul and Barnabas were not immune. First, they were met with opposition in Paphos where they came upon a dishonest Jewish sorcerer, or wizard, named Barjesus (also called Elymas). The city's deputy (or governor) Sergius Paulus welcomed Paul and Barnabas to come and share the gospel, desiring "to hear the word of God" (Acts 13:7 KJV).

Howver, Elymas diverted and blocked them from preaching the gospel, "seeking to turn away the deputy from the faith" (Acts 13:8 KJV).

But Paul, filled with the Holy Spirit, looked Elymas in the eye and called him the son of the devil. He asked the sorcerer, "O full of all subtilty and all mischief, thou child of the devil, thou enemy of all righteousness, wilt thou not cease to pervert the right ways of the Lord?"

(Acts 13:10 KJV). Paul told Elymas the hand of the Lord was upon Elymas, and he would be blinded (Acts 13:11). Immediately the sorcerer went blind and looked for someone to guide him around. When the deputy saw this, Scripture says, he was "astonished at the doctrine of the Lord," (Acts 13:12 KJV) and put his faith in Jesus.

Paul and Barnabas were not experts in dealing with sorcerers, but the Holy Spirit equipped them for the task they had been called to.

Equipped for Service to All

Leaving Paphos, the two headed for Perga. At that point for some unknown reason John Mark quit and went back to Jerusalem (Acts 13:13), while Paul and Barnabas continued.

On the Sabbath, they went to the synagogue where the ruler of the synagogue asked them if they had words of encouragement. Paul stood up and gave a history lesson surveying the Hebrews' captivity in Egypt, King David's rule, and John the Baptist's ministry—all the way to Jesus. He of course, detailed the mission, ministry and murder of Jesus and His resurrection. Paul ended his sermon declaring God raised Jesus Christ from the dead just as the psalmist prophesied in the Scriptures: "Thou art my Son, this day have I begotten thee" (Acts 13:33 KJV).

He then told those who were listening that because Jesus lives, forgiveness of sins was available to anyone who believe. Jesus accomplished everything that the law of Moses could never accomplish. When the service was

over, "Paul and Barnabas were invited back to preach
again the next Sabbath" (Acts 13:42 MSG). Many Jews
and converts to Judaism agreed with the message and
encouraged Paul and Barnabas to "continue in the grace
of God (Acts 13:43 KJV).

The next week practically the whole city showed up
to hear the Word of God. But the Jews were filled with
jealousy and tried to discredit Paul, contradicting and
blaspheming him (Acts 13:45). But Paul and Barnabas
didn't back down. They stood their ground and declared:

> It was necessary that the word of God should first have
> been spoken to you: but seeing ye put it from you, and
> judge yourselves unworthy of everlasting life, lo, we turn to
> the Gentiles. — *Acts 13:46 (KJV)*

Because the Jews were prideful and stiff-necked, Paul
and Barnabas announced they would turning to the
gentiles who would receive the message the Jews would
not embrace.

When the gentiles heard this, they were happy and
filled with joy and many of them accepted the gift of
eternal life through Jesus Christ because of the Word.
The message of salvation spread like wildfire, while
some of the Jews convinced affluent townspeople that
the gospel was a threat to their way of life. They began
to turn on Paul and Barnabas, eventually forcing them to
leave. Not swayed, Paul and Barnabas shrugged their
shoulders and went on to the next town, Iconium,
"brimming with joy and the Holy Spirit, two happy
disciples" (Acts 13:52 MSG).

Likely Paul and Barnabas expected their own people would have received the message of the gospel with joy—but instead, it was a people they were not expecting who received the message. They did not need to adjust their gospel message, but simply share how Jesus transformed their own life. The Holy Spirit equipped them for the job at hand, even sharing with a people who were different from them culturally, religiously, and ethnically—and lives were saved.

Set Apart for God's Assignments

When the church prays, the Holy Spirit speaks. The Holy Spirit designated and separated Paul and Barnabas for a specific assignment to the gentiles. The word 'separate' is the Greek word *aphorizo*, which means "to mark off from others by boundaries, to limit, or to separate."[35]

Aphorizo carries a similar meaning the Greek word *hagiazō*, which means "to separate from profane things and dedicate to God." *Hagiazō* means to set apart for a divine task.[36] God through the agency of the Holy Spirit gives assignments. Everyone does not have the same assignment, and divine assignments are not an individual believer's decision but rather their discovery. Writing to the Corinthians church Paul said:

> *Now there are diversities of gifts, but the same Spirit. And there are differences of administrations, but the same Lord. And there are diversities of operations, but it is the same God which worketh all in all. But the manifestation of the*

Spirit is given to every man to profit withal. — *1 Corinthians 12:4–7 (KJV)*

The Holy Spirit determines the areas that a person is gifted in to best serve the church of Jesus Christ. The Spirit gives followers of Jesus assurance and assistance, and will strengthen them when attacked.

Assignment Assurance

Barnabas and Paul waxed bold as they encountered constant opposition. The Holy Spirit sent them on an assignment and gave them the confidence and assurance they needed. In the face of opposition with Barjesus, Acts 13:9 says Paul was "filled with the Holy Ghost" (KJV).

The power of the Spirit that guided the early church is described by the phrase, "the filling" (cf. 2:4; 4:8, 31; 6:3; 7:55; 9:17; 13:9, 52). The ongoing, daily filling of the Spirit is the normal state of all believers (cf. Ephesians 5:18). In Acts, it is usually associated with a boldness and clarity to proclaim the gospel.

So, too, should the church today depend on the Holy Spirit. When believers are daily filled with the Spirit, speaking the truth of the gospel will be a natural experience that is expressed with audacity and precision. They will be assured that the message that goes out will be exactly what God wants communicated.

Assignment Assistance

When Paul and Barnabas preached in the synagogues, the Holy Spirit placed people in their lives to encourage them as seen Acts 14:43. The book of Hebrews calls believers to "exhort one another daily, while it is called To day; lest any of you be hardened through the deceitfulness of sin" (Hebrews 3:13 KJV). As such, it is important to encourage the body of Christ, that believers might press on in the work God has called them to do.

In the same way, the Holy Spirit will provide support when you need it, as well. Sometimes it will be through another person, and sometimes it will be a spiritual spurring on—an unexplainable sense of His presence and the ability to press on. The Holy Spirit is called "the helper," (also translated 'advocate' or 'comforter') in John 14:26 and Romans 8:26. The Greek word for 'helper' is the word *paraklētos*, which means "summoned, called to one's side, called to one's aid."[37] This is one of the most powerful roles of the Holy Spirit—to come alongside God's people to help them in the ministry of the Word.

Strength When Attacked

Finally, the Holy Spirit does allow God's assignments to come under attack. One of the hardest aspects of divine assignments is when people try to assassinate your character and cause. However, Paul and Barnabas shrugged off the attack and kept moving forward.

Paul and Barnabas experienced attacks from workers of iniquity in Acts 13. There is a difference between sin and iniquity. 'Iniquity' means "premeditated choice, continuing without repentance."[38] Jesus had strong words for workers of iniquity in Matthew 7:21–23:

> *Not every one that saith unto me, Lord, Lord, shall enter into the kingdom of heaven; but he that doeth the will of my Father which is in heaven. Many will say to me in that day, Lord, Lord, have we not prophesied in thy name? and in thy name have cast out devils? and in thy name done many wonderful works? And then will I profess unto them, I never knew you: depart from me, ye that work iniquity.*
> *(KJV)*

The Holy Spirit and God's Word

The Word of God changes lives and it is the assignment of those who are called to deliver it to proclaim it.

At the end of Acts 13 many gentiles received eternal life through the message of salvation delivered by the preachers—they delivered the truth of the Word of God, and lives were changed. Paul thanked the Thessalonians, for he said, "when you received the word of God, which you heard from us, you accepted it not as a human word, but as it actually is, the word of God, which is indeed at work in you who believe" (1 Thessalonians 2:13 NIV).

The Holy Spirit is the author of Scripture and therefore, when the church preaches the Word, God says, "It will not return to me empty, but will accomplish what

I desire and achieve for the purpose for which I sent it" (Isaiah 55:11 NIV).

CHAPTER FOURTEEN

Power, Perseverance, Partnership, and Prudence

Acts 14

Long time therefore abode they speaking boldly in the Lord, which gave testimony unto the word of his grace, and granted signs and wonders to be done by their hands. But the multitude of the city was divided: and part held with the Jews, and part with the apostles.

And when there was an assault made both of the Gentiles, and also of the Jews with their rulers, to use them despitefully, and to stone them. — Acts 14:3–5 (KJV)

Is opposition worth continuing in ministry? Chapter 13 revealed Paul and Barnabas faced quite a bit of opposition—enough to cause many today to rethink ministry or even quit. Opposition is inevitable. Jesus faced it, the apostles faced it, and disciples of Christ today will face it. However, the Holy Spirit is fighting with God's committed servants to cause the gospel to go out despite the forces of evil that are trying to prevent this from happening.

The early church movement grew because of a few committed followers of Jesus who held fast to the assignment given to them.

The Apostles' Opposition Intensifies

While in Iconium, the Paul and Barnabas faced more opposition. When they first arrived, they immediately went to the synagogue and began to preach the message of the gospel (Acts 14:1). They started a ministry. Iconium was a good city to plant the seeds of the gospel.

The name 'Iconium' comes from the Greek word *Ikonion*, which means "Little Image." It is from the root word *eikōn*, where the English word 'icon' comes from. It has been described as a rich city with many beliefs and superstitions.[39] In Acts 14:2, problems start for Paul and Barnabas.

The unbelieving Jews "stirred up the Gentiles, and made their minds evil affected against the brethren" (Acts 14:2 KJV). The words 'made' and 'evil affected' are both translated from one Greek word, *kakoō. Kakoō* means "to embitter, to exasperate."[40] The apostle's enemies in Iconium soured others against Paul and Barnabas and the new converts. However, Paul and Barnabas stayed a long time in Iconium preaching the "word of grace" as the Holy Spirit "granted signs and wonders to be done by their hands" to validate their claims (Acts 14:3 KJV). However, "the multitude of the city was divided" (Acts 14:4 KJV). Opposition had taken root, and was beginning to grow.

The two apostles learned of a plot to incite a riot and to have Paul and Barnabas stoned. They escaped to the next city, remained quiet for a time, and then continued with the ministry of the Word. While in Lystra, a crippled man was healed by the power of the Holy Spirit through Paul's very voice:

> *There sat a certain man at Lystra, impotent in his feet, being a cripple from his mother's womb, who never had walked: The same heard Paul speak: who stedfastly beholding him, and perceiving that he had faith to be healed, Said with a loud voice, Stand upright on thy feet. And he leaped and walked.* — *Acts 14:8–10 (KJV)*

The crowds responded with praise, believing gods had come down "in the likeness of men" (Acts 14:11 KJV). They called Barnabas "Jupiter" and Paul "Mercurius" (Acts 14:12) and were about to offer sacrifices to the two! But the apostles stopped the crowds, and explained that they were mere men who came with the gospel message to turn them to the living God who created all things, and away from godless superstitions (Acts 14:15).

The Jews from Iconium had followed Paul and Barnabas, turned the crowds against the apostles, and stoned Paul leaving him for dead. The crowd was easily swayed—one minute lifting them up as gods and the next, beating Paul unconscious. The next day, however, Paul rose and continued to Derbe with Barnabas to preach the gospel. After they preached in Derbe, they returned to Lystra, Iconiumm, and Antioch (Acts 14:21).

The apostle returned to these cities to encourage the growth of the believers and to exhort them to continue in the faith. They warned them that they "must through much tribulation enter into the kingdom of God" (Acts 14:22 KJV). It is insufficient to be redeemed but not continue to grow and mature in the faith. When a new convert comes to Jesus, they must be taught what it means to grow in the faith. As they "work out their salvation," they will begin to be transformed into Christ's image. Paul made this clear in his letter to the Romans, stating: "For those God foreknew he also predestined to be conformed to the image of his Son" (Romans 8:29 NIV). He also wrote, "He is the one we proclaim, admonishing and teaching everyone with all wisdom, so that we may present everyone fully mature in Christ" (Colossians 1:28 NIV). Maturity in Christ was their goal, and Paul and Barnabas did not shy from teaching believers how important this was for the growth of the church.

Paul and Barnabas "ordained them elders in every church," prayed and fasted, and commissioned all who believed to the Lord (Acts 14:23 KJV). New churches were now established in Lystra, Iconium, and Antioch.

Paul and Barnabas left, catching a ship to Antioch where the church started. There they shared testimonies of "how God had used them to throw the door of faith wide open so people of all nations could come streaming in (Acts 14:27–28 MSG).

Faith Accessible to All

The King James Version of Acts 14:27 says that God had "opened the door of faith unto the Gentiles" (KJV). This suggests both the opening of a door that had been first confined to the Jews, and the introduction of the gospel to the distant gentiles through that door into the church. Before this, faith was inaccessible to the gentiles. Ephesians 2:12 says regarding the gentiles, "That at that time ye were without Christ, being aliens from the commonwealth of Israel, and stranger from the covenants of the promise, having no hope, and without God in the world" (KJV).

Now that the preachers had been sent out to the gentiles, the door was open, and faith was accessible to all. Churches were established in many cities, and members were established in the faith. And the movement continued to swell.

Perfectly Supplied

The Holy Spirit supplied everything the apostles needed in Acts 14. He gave the apostles the power to preach, enabled them to persevere, provided partners for ministry, and discernment to know when the ministry would cause more harm then help.

Power to Preach

Chapter 14 reveals there was opposition not only in Iconium, but everywhere Paul And Barnabus preached.

Yet they continued to speak God's gospel with boldness. Galatians 5:17 says that man's sinful nature and the Holy Spirit are "forces [that] are constantly fighting each other, so you are not free to carry out your good intentions." Though this verse is speaking of the tension in individuals as they push against their sinful nature, the concept is true for anyone who has stepped out as a witness for Jesus. The enemy will come against the work of the Holy Spirit, and the church must not only be aware of this but fight against it.

The power of the Holy Spirit gave Paul and Barnabas the ability to push past the opposition they experienced in every city they visited.

Perseverance

Paul and Barnabas continued to preach the gospel with boldness in spite of the opposition it caused. This is the hallmark of Acts 14. While the enemies of God were working hard to taint the people's minds, Paul and Barnabas continued to preach to counter the work of the enemy—and in the end God was victorious. However, the price was weighty; Paul and Barnabas experienced intense persecution—even stoning! They were aware of the plots to hurt them but still persevered.

So too will the Spirit enable the church to persevere today.

THE MOVEMENT IN ACTS · 149

Partnership

Not everyone who heard the gospel message of grace believed; some came against Paul and Barnabas. But others came alongside them, caring enough about the ministry to warn them of impending danger so they would have time to flee.

It is important to pay attention to those whom the Lord surround the church with—to both encourage and to warn.

Prudence

The situation escalated to the point where Paul and Barnabas had to leave. This was not a sign of weakness but the Holy Spirit gave them prudence, or discernment to know when their ministry would cause more harm then help. Moving on is not an admission of fault or failure, as the opposition will falsely say is the case; sometimes it's the Holy Spirit supplying the wisdom to move on. Matthew 10:14 says, "If anyone will not welcome you or listen to your words, leave that home or town and shake the dust off your feet" (NIV). Not everyone will welcome the truth of the gospel message, and there is a time when it's okay to move on.

The work of the gospel is not easy, and few carry on like Paul and Barnabas. Many quit at the first sign of fatigue, difficulty, danger, or criticism. However, consider the miraculous growth of the movement of the church when two men committed to persevere, even to death, to spread the Word. Through their obedience and empowered by the Spirit the Word of God went out.

Rest assured the Holy Spirit is still operating today and will supply power, perseverance, partnership, and prudence for the ministry you have been called to. Then, hold fast to the assignment until the Holy Spirit says you are finished.

CHAPTER FIFTEEN

Setting Standards for the Saints

Acts 15

But there rose up certain of the sect of the Pharisees which believed, saying, That it was needful to circumcise them, and to command them to keep the law of Moses. And the apostles and elders came together for to consider of this matter.

And when there had been much disputing, Peter rose up, and said unto them, Men and brethren, ye know how that a good while ago God made choice among us, that the Gentiles by my mouth should hear the word of the gospel, and believe.

And God, which knoweth the hearts, bare them witness, giving them the Holy Ghost, even as he did unto us; And put no difference between us and them, purifying their hearts by faith. — Acts 15:5–9 (KJV)

As the church continued to grow, conflict shifted from outside of the church to within the church as disagreements between believers surfaced. They began to dispute the requirements for salvation. For centuries Jews had circumcised males, as a sign of their covenant with God. This issue of circumcision was something Jewish believers thought gentiles must keep as well.

Though something that could have divided the church, the Holy Spirit navigated the situation.

The Conflict Begins

Men came from Judea to Antioch and challenged the salvation of gentile converts because they were not circumcised "after the manner of Moses" (Acts 15:1 KJV). The word 'manner' in Acts 15:1 is translated from the Greek word *ethos*, which means "a custom" or "law, institute, prescription or rite."[41]

These men felt gentile male converts should be circumcised after baptism to to be saved because the law required it. Paul and Barnabas were instructed to go back to the church in Jerusalem to confer with the apostles and elders on this matter.

Though many Pharisees fought against Christianity, some Pharisees believed. These believers, however, held fast to pharisaical traditions and rose up declaring it was a requirement for gentiles to be circumcised and keep the law of Moses. These Pharisees were not only advocating circumcision but keeping the entire law of Moses (Acts 15:1).

However, Peter intervened—reminding the Pharisees of how God says a person is saved.

The Gospel of Salvation

Peter rose and spoke boldly about God's vision for the church (Acts 15:7). He recapped the council of how God chose him to be the spokesman to the gentiles and how the preaching of the gospel would save them. God gave the gentiles the Holy Spirit just as He had given it to the Jews—making no distinction and purifying their hearts by faith (Acts 15:9; see also Acts 10). Peter rebuked the believing Pharisees for trying to inject the law that they couldn't even carry out.

Jesus addressed this issue in Matthew 23:2-4:

> *Saying The scribes and the Pharisees sit in Moses' seat: All therefore whatsoever they bid you observe, that observe and do; but do not ye after their works: for they say, and do not. For they bind heavy burdens and grievous to be borne, and lay them on men's shoulders; but they themselves will not move them with one of their fingers.* — **Matthew 23:2–4 (KJV)**

Peter referred to the law as a "yoke" in Acts 15:10: "Why tempt ye God, to put a yoke upon the neck of the disciples, which neither our fathers nor we were able to bear?" (KJV) he questioned. The English word 'yoke' in this verse is a translation from the Greek word *zygos* which refers to a piece of wood that is fastened on the neck of a beast of burden. In a metaphorical sense, it is used to describe the effect on a person of rules that are impossible to keep, "of troublesome laws imposed on one—especially of the Mosaic law."[42]

The apostle figuratively compared keeping the law to slavery. The law was a set of rules no person could keep—those who tried were like slaves to that law. He concluded that all people are saved by the grace of God through Jesus Christ (Acts 15:11). After Peter spoke there was a period of silence before Paul and Barnabas began to speak giving confirmation through their own testimonies.

James, the brother of Jesus followed, affirming that what Peter preached lined up with the words of the prophets. He quoted the prophet Amos as evidence of God's existing plan for the gentiles:

> *After this I will return, and will build again the tabernacle of David, which is fallen down; and I will build again the ruins thereof, and I will set it up: That the residue of men might seek after the Lord, and all the Gentiles, upon whom my name is called, saith the Lord, who doeth all these things.* — *Acts 15:16–17 (KJV)*

Finally, James announced the conclusion of the matter: adult gentile men did not have to undergo circumcision.

God's Standard for the Gentiles

James set a standard for the gentiles. He did this because the gentiles were used to a life and culture centered on idolatry. As new creations in Christ, the gentiles were now held to a new standard—but they had to be instructed as to what that standard entailed.

The four resulting requirements upon the gentiles are known as *halakah* in Judaism. *Halakah* is a Hebrew word that literally means "the path one walks."[43] It is more simply known as Jewish law.

Each of these requirements was based on ancient conditions found in the law of Moses for a stranger or foreigner who desired to live among the tribes of Israel (see Leviticus 17 and 18). James began addressing the most common sins committed, based on the gentiles' pagan culture. Though the gentiles would not fall under the Mosaic system since they were by descent not Jewish, they would be asked to do certain things that would initiate their Christian growth and line up with a new way of life. James concluded gentiles were to "abstain from meats offered to idols, and from blood, and from the things strangled, and from fornication" (Acts 15:29 KJV).

Most if not all of the converts to Christianity were coming out of pagan religions, so the message for gentiles was to break away from their old pagan way of life.

Eating Food Sacrificed to Idols: Leviticus 17:3–9

Animals were being sacrificed to demons outside the camp instead of to God and then later sold for purchase. This was a normal way of life for the gentile but offensive to the Jewish Christian. God set this standard for any foreigner who would attach themselves to Israel, thousands of years before Christ. Through Moses God had said, "And they shall no more offer their sacrifices unto devils, after whom they have gone a whoring. This shall be a statute for ever unto them throughout their generations" (Leviticus 17:7 KJV). This Old Testament requirement for foreigners was where James drew his conclusions for first-century gentile believers. James's command was to avoid food that had been sacrificed for demonic reasons.

Sexual Immorality: Leviticus 18

Adultery, incest, homosexuality, and bestiality were part of pagan religion in the first century—and clearly an issue during the time of Moses. God addressed these morality issues in Leviticus 18. Of these detestable practices God said:

> *Defile not ye yourselves in any of these things: for in all these the nations are defiled which I cast out before you: And the land is defiled: therefore I do visit the iniquity thereof upon it, and the land itself vomiteth out her inhabitants. Ye shall therefore keep my statutes and my judgments, and shall not commit any of these abominations; neither any of your own nation, nor any stranger that sojourneth among you.* — **Leviticus 18:24–26 (KJV)**

God forbid both the foreigner and the Israelite in ancient biblical times from participating in incest, homosexuality, adultery, and bestiality. Thus, the apostles surmised these morality requirements had not changed; gentiles were required to abide by God's instruction in this area of sexual purity (Acts 15:6–23).

Eating Meat of Strangled Animals: Leviticus 17:15–16

Both the Israelites and foreigners were required in the Old Testament to refrain from eating animals that had died naturally or had been killed by wild beasts. An animal that had been strangled, died naturally, or had been killed by wild beasts did not yet have its blood properly drained from its body. Thus, gentiles in the New Testament should not eat the meat of strangled animals, either.

Eating Blood: Leviticus 17:10–14

Finally, the command to abstain from eating blood was based on Leviticus 17:10-14 (see also Genesis 9:4; Leviticus 3:17; 7:26–27; 19:26; Deuteronomy 12:16, 23; 15:23). Neither Israelites nor outsiders to the covenant were allowed to eat the blood of an animal, because blood sustains the life of the flesh (Genesis 9:4; Leviticus 17:11, 14; Deuteronomy 12:23).

Though there is liberty in Christ, these were strict requirements for gentile converts.

Separate for the Sake of the Gospel

Barnabas wanted to take John Mark along with them on the next missionary journey. But Paul disagreed with the idea. John Mark had deserted the ministry team in Pamphylia, and this was a concern for Paul. The Bible says, "the contention was so sharp between them, that they departed asunder one from the other: and so, Barnabas took Mark, and sailed unto Cyprus" (Acts 15:39 KJV).

In Acts 15:39 the word 'contention' (also translated 'sharp') is the Greek word *paroxysmos*, which means "an incitement," or "irritation."[44] It is a medical term to describe a sharp increase in the intensity of a disease. Here it means that the disagreement between Paul and Barnabas became so strong they parted one from another. Although Barnabas and John Mark departed from Paul, the three men still carried out the work on separate but respective journeys.

Even with this disagreement, the work of the gospel continued; in fact, Barnabas, John Mark, and Paul appear to have reconciled. In 2 Timothy 4:11 Paul charged Timothy with the task of finding John Mark: "Take Mark, and bring him with thee: for he is profitable to me for the ministry" (KJV) (see also Colossians 4:10).

Conflict and the Holy Spirit

Conflict within the church is not necessarily a bad thing. In fact, the Holy Spirit often uses it to further His work of expanding God's Kingdom.

The Holy Spirit Clears Up Controversial Issues

Controversy is one of the enemy's tactics against the church. There are no recorded examples of people coming to faith in Antioch during Paul's and Barnabas's time there—because of controversy.

The Holy Spirit is not the author of confusion. In this instance, the Holy Spirit allowed differences of opinions to surface on the premise that clarity would ultimately come about through His guidance.

The letters to the gentiles in Antioch in Acts 15:23 stated church leaders were aware some men had come from their main church in Jerusalem and confused them about circumcision. "We gave no such commandment," they wrote (Acts 15:24 KJV). These letters, delivered by Judas, Silas, Barnabas, and Paul (Acts 24, 27) assured the gentiles they did not have to be circumcised but also gave them instructions on what to abstain from.

Thus, through controversy, the Holy Spirit set standards that would be necessary for the church to continue growing, and to remain healthy and set apart from pagan religions.

There are a number of roles the Holy Spirit plays in regard to controversy within the church.

The Holy Spirit Positions Leaders to Investigate

Paul and Barnabas were sent back to Jerusalem to meet with the apostles and the church to investigate the matter at hand.

Believers must trust the Holy Spirit for the right outcome through the leaders He has put in position. The council meeting in Jerusalem was crucial for the plight of Christianity as it relates to grace and legalism. The church could have forever been split but the Holy Spirit used key players to resolve the conflict.

The Holy Spirit Provides Scripture as an Authority:

James was able to provide the scriptural basis for God's plan of salvation for gentiles citing prophecy from Amos. As conflict arises within the church, the first thing leaders should do is consider whether God has given instruction in His Word for how to handle the situation.

The Holy Spirit Establishes Standards as a Paradigm

The gentiles in Antioch came from a culture that offered idols to Satan, drank blood, and practiced sex as a religion. Therefore, James gave them a model, or paradigm, to live by. If there were no models to follow, followers of Jesus could set their own standards—what is today called humanism, or living by human standards. The Holy Spirit sets the standards for both Jews and gentiles.

As the church grew, the source of conflict shifted. It had previously come from the unbelieving world, but in Acts 15 evolved to conflict within the church—primarily with the issue of circumcision. However, the Holy Spirit who knows all things was not unaware, and used this conflict to further the Kingdom of God.

Because of controversy, the Holy Spirit set standards that would be paramount for the church to continue growing, and to remain healthy and set apart from pagan religions. Just as in the first century, believers today must trust the Holy Spirit for the right outcome through the leaders He has put in position to deal with conflict and controversy.

Ultimately, the Holy Spirit uses everything to move the church toward harmony—to bringing peace where there is discord, by setting standards, and sometimes by separating people or ministries for the sake of growth of the church.

CHAPTER SIXTEEN

The Holy Navigator

Acts 16

And after he had seen the vision, immediately we endeavoured to go into Macedonia, assuredly gathering that the Lord had called us for to preach the gospel unto them. — Acts 16:10 (KJV)

The Holy Spirit does always reveal the future clearly, but He always reveals the next step. In Acts 16, Paul had began his second missionary journey. Timothy, Silas, and Luke were travelling with him, and the Holy Spirit was present as their navigator. To 'navigate' means "to steer a course through a medium," as in sailing a boat.[45]

Like the captain of a ship, the Holy Spirit controlled Paul and his associates' course. He used different means including restrictions, visions, directions, restlessness, revival, and resolve to steer the apostles to where they were supposed to be.

The Gospel Spreads

Restrictions

Paul and Silas thought it was best to go to Asia Minor, but the Holy Spirit prevented them from using that route; Scripture says, "but the Spirit suffered them not" (Acts 16:7 KJV). It is not clear what the roadblock was, only that there was some sort of obstruction, physical or spiritual. Perhaps a literal road was blocked or maybe it was opposition from Jews. Regardless, the Holy Spirit navigated Paul and Silas by restricting their movement.

Revelation

One night Paul had a vision of a man praying and pleading for he and Silas to come and help them in Macedonia. Paul awoke knowing the Spirit was leading him to continue to Macedonia: it was time to preach to the people to what is today Europe.

This was a major step in the movement of the church. When Paul went to Macedonia he took the gospel from one continent to another. At this point, Christianity was no longer an Eastern religion but had spread to the West. The Holy Spirit often navigates through dreams and visions.

Directions

The first convert Paul interacted with in Macedonia was a woman named Lydia. Led by the Holy Spirit, the ministry team went down by the riverside; they had heard there was a prayer meeting in progress. There they encountered Lydia. She was "a seller of purple, of the city of Thyatira, which worshipped God" (Acts 16:14 KJV).

However, she did not know Jesus. Acts 14 says when she heard him speaking she "attended unto the things which were spoken of Paul" (Acts 16:14 KJV). Lydia opened her heart to God and was baptized along with her household. Paul and Silas remained at her house because of her hospitality.

Sometimes the Holy Spirit navigates ministry teams to specific locations for purposes they can't quite see— in this case, a riverside.

Restlessness and Revival

Sometime later, Paul and Silas became restless with the behavior of a little slave girl who had psychic powers and had been following Paul. After several days, Paul rebuked the spirit saying, "I command thee in the name of Jesus Christ to come out of her" (Acts 16:18 KJV). Scripture said the evil spirit came out of her that same hour. Her masters were angry because she was their "moneymaker." They lured Paul and Silas into the marketplace, brought them before the rulers of the city, and stirred up the people against them. Paul and Silas

166 · OSCAR T. MOSES

were thrown into prison (Acts 16:24). They were placed in maximum security with steel leg irons clamped on their legs (Acts 16:24 MSG).

While in jail, Paul and Silas were moved by the Spirit to pray and sing. The other prisoners heard them (Acts 16:25). At midnight, an earthquake shook the jail cell. The door opened and the leg clamps fell off (Acts 16:26). The jailer awoke to find the jail door opened and assumed Paul and Silas had escaped—and subsequently drew a sword to kill himself.

But Paul stopped him and declared:

> *Do thyself no harm: for we are all here. Then he called for a light, and sprang in, and came trembling, and fell down before Paul and Silas, and brought them out, and said, Sirs, what must I do to be saved? And they said, believe on the Lord Jesus Christ, and thou shalt be saved, and thy house. — Acts 16:28–31 (KJV)*

The Holy Spirit directed Paul and Silas to the slave girl, which led to their imprisonment. Their imprisonment led to the miracle of their release, which moved the jailer to believe.

The Holy Spirit sometimes navigates believers through restlessness, and many times it is through restlessness revival begins.

Resolve

At daybreak, the judge released Paul and Silas saying, "Let those men go" (Acts 16:35 KJV). But Paul wouldn't budge. He responded, "They have beaten us openly uncondemned, being Romans, and have cast us into prison; and now do they thrust us out privily? nay verily; but let them come themselves and fetch us out" (Acts 16:27 KJV). The court judges did not know Paul and Silas were Roman citizens and that they wrongly had condemned them. They immediately apologized and asked the two men to leave the city. Upon their release, Paul and Silas stopped by Lydia's house to encourage the church in the faith—and then went on their way (Acts 16:40).

The Holy Spirit carried Paul and Silas to a brief imprisonment, but promptly orchestrated their release and moved them on to another direction. The church must be prepared for the movement of the Holy Spirit, and welcome quick moves that may not make sense.

In each situation in Acts 15, Paul and Silas could have responded in their flesh—staying when they should leave or leaving when they should stay. However, they obeyed God, and the church continued to grow. Matthew 7:21 says, "Not every one that saith unto me, Lord, Lord, shall enter into the kingdom of heaven; but he that doeth the will of my Father which is in heaven" (KJV). The church grows when its members are willing to obey God—to do the will of the father even when it doesn't make sense.

Movement also occurs when its least expected. When circumstances change, embrace those changes and wait for what is ahead that might seem unclear. Romans 8:28 says, "all things work together for good to them that love God, to them who are the called according to his purpose" (KJV). Remember this promise when things look messy and it seems God has turned His back. Likely He is doing something profound for the Kingdom, but the pieces of the puzzle aren't clear yet.

Finally, understand that the Holy Spirit knows best. John the apostle wrote, "Howbeit when he, the Spirit of truth, is come, he will guide you into all truth: for he shall not speak of himself; but whatsoever he shall hear, that shall he speak: and he will shew you things to come" (John 16:13 KJV).

God will reveal just enough of things to come

to give you confidence in taking the next step. The Holy Spirit will navigate and guide those who are committed to obeying Him!

CHAPTER SEVENTEEN

The Holy Spirit Reasons

Acts 17

And they took him, and brought him unto Areopagus, saying, May we know what this new doctrine, whereof thou speakest, is? For thou bringest certain strange things to our ears: we would know therefore what these things mean.
— *Acts 17:19–20 (KJV)*

The Holy Spirit meets people where they are, to lead them where they need to go. Sometimes a person makes the decision to believe in Jesus based on an emotional response, simply by hearing the gospel and believing in their heart. However, others need to come to a place of faith using intellectual reasoning—making sure what they are believing makes sense in their mind. This is what happened when Paul and Silas continued their ministry to Greece—with Thessalonians, Bereans, and Athenians.

In Acts 17, Scripture reveals how the Holy Spirit empowered Paul and Silas to present the gospel effectively to different groups. Through reasoning, the apostles were able to provide proof that the gospel of Jesus Christ was true. The Holy Spirit stirred people to consider from a factual standpoint if what the apostles preached was true.

Reasoning with the Scriptures

In Thessalonica

The Holy Spirit empowered Paul and Silas to reason, explain, give evidence and proclaim the Messiahship of Jesus Christ for three Sabbaths in Thessalonica, a town in Greece (Act 17:2). Hard-lined Jews had become overwhelmed with jealousy because many Jews were believing Jesus was the Messiah.

Thus, they assembled a band of brawlers to hunt Paul and Silas down—arresting Jason believing he was hiding the two men. Jason and his friends were brought before the city fathers and accused of assisting the apostle in destroying the world with new doctrines which were an affront to Caesar. To rival Caesar's greatness was one of the most severe crimes one could commit in the Roman Empire. However, they received divine help from some brothers in Christ, who sent them to Berea to meet with the Jewish community there (Acts 12:10).

In Berea

Paul and Silas escaped to the Jewish community living in Berea, in northern Greece. The Holy Spirit encouraged the Bereans. They had received Paul's words with an open mind, but sought out God's Word to see if what Paul said aligned with Scripture:

> *These were more noble than those in Thessalonica, in that they received the word with all readiness of mind, and searched the scriptures daily, whether those things were so.*
> — *Acts 17:11 (KJV)*

Paul made note of the difference in the Berean's response to the gospel—calling them "more noble" than the Thessalonians. The Bereans were excited to hear the Word of God. The Bereans exhibited two characteristics that affected the church movement in that town.

First, they received the Word with all readiness. The Bereans heard Paul speak and accepted it as God's Word—evidence that God's Spirit was within them and working. However, they didn't just take what Paul said as gospel. They corroborated his word with the Scriptures to find out whether these things were so...and they did so "daily" (Acts 17:11 KJV).

However, the unbelieving Jews from Thessalonica found out Paul and Silas were in Berea and promptly sought to find them. They "stirred up the people" (Acts 17:13 KJV). Paul and Silas slipped out and caught a boat to Athens leaving Timothy and Silas behind.

In Athens

The Holy Spirit enlightened the citizens in Athens, too. Athens was a city in southern Greece experiencing a period of decline, though it was still recognized as a center of culture and education. The glory of politics and commerce Athens was known for was fading.

In the first century, Athens was a city populated by cultured pagans and its people were devoted to philosophy. Paul and Silas encountered a "junkyard of idols" (Acts 17:16 MSG) that Athenians worshipped, and disputed these false idols daily with the citizens. Certain philosophers of the Epicureans, and of the Stoics, encountered Paul.

Epicureans believed God had no interest in humanity and the main purpose of life was pleasure. They acknowledged gods only in name. They were materialists. Epicureans declared, "enjoy life!"[46]

Stoics, on the other hand, believed the goal in life was to rise above all things and show no emotion to either pain or pleasure. They did not deny God but they were pantheists that believed life is determined by fate. Rather than "enjoying life," the Stoics said, "endure life."[47]

Some of these Epicureans and Stoics questioned, "What will this babbler say?" (Acts 17:18 KJV) Others commented, "He seemeth to be a setter forth of strange gods: because he preached unto them Jesus, and the resurrection" (Acts 17:18 KJV). So, they took him, and brought him unto Areopagus, saying, "May we know what this new doctrine, whereof thou speakest, is?" (Acts 17:19 KJV).

Through reasoning, Paul proceeded to present a logical argument using strong persuasion under divine authority of the Holy Spirit.

Areopagus

Acts 17:19 says, "And they took him, and brought him unto Areopagus" (KJV). The Areopagus was the council that had charge of religious and educational matters. It was a court on Mars' Hill, where philosophy was given a platform. Here the Epicureans and Stoics allowed Paul to reason with them about Jesus Christ.

Paul told them they were too superstitious and challenged their faith (Acts 17:22) He told the crowd how he encountered an altar erected "TO THE UNKNOWN GOD" (Acts 17:23 KJV).

Paul enlightened them to what the "Unknown God" was. He began with the majesty of God and expounded on the movement of humanity (Acts 17:28). He concluded with the Messiahship of Jesus Christ. Paul proclaimed to these intellects that they now knew God and God was calling them to change. When Paul presented Jesus Christ as the resurrected savior, some left immediately. Some mocked him, and others wanted to hear more (Acts 17:32).

Through Paul the Holy Spirit transformed Dionysus the Areopagite and a woman named Damaris who was in the crowd. Though the masses did not accept Christ, the Holy Spirit empowered Paul to reason among Athens's intellectual elite—who respected him

"God calls us to be salt, to be light, not to make believers. Only God can open a closed heart and blind eyes and deaf ears."[48]

Power, Proof, Reason, and a Pathway

The Holy Spirit emboldens believers to present the gospel to different people, regardless of academic, religious, or social background: "For it is the power of God unto salvation to every one that believeth; to the Jew first, and also to the Greek" (Romans 1:16 KJV). The Holy Spirit also provides proof of the truth of the gospel, through the Scriptures. The Bereans experienced this by lining Paul's words up with the Word of God. This is what it means to "Study to shew thyself approved unto God, a workman that needeth not to be ashamed, rightly dividing the word of truth" (2 Timothy 2:15 KJV).

The Holy Spirit also appeals to people through reasoning, by identifying sin. Isiaah 1:18 says, "Come now, and let us reason together, saith the LORD: though your sins be as scarlet, they shall be as white as snow; though they be red like crimson, they shall be as wool" (Isaiah 1:18 KJV). Finally, the Holy Spirit provides a pathway to salvation. Jesus is "the way, the truth, and the life: no man cometh unto the Father, but by me" (John 14:6 KJV).

CHAPTER EIGHTEEN

Affirmation, Assurance, and Assistance

Acts 18

Then spake the Lord to Paul in the night by a vision, Be not afraid, but speak, and hold not thy peace: For I am with thee, and no man shall set on thee to hurt thee: for I have much people in this city. And he continued there a year and six months, teaching the word of God among them. — Acts 18:9–11 (KJV)

The Holy Spirit does not always remove opposition but will give that which is needed to complete what has been assigned. While in Corinth, the Holy Spirit affirmed and assured, Paul, while assisting others by correcting teaching that was not quite accurate.

The Gospel in Corinth

Paul left Athens and traveled to Corinth, a large city known for its trade and commerce. It was located by a seaport, which made it accommodating to neighboring cities.

Upon his arrival at Corinth he found Aquila, a Jew from Pontus, and his wife Priscilla (Acts 18:1). Aquila, Priscilla and Paul shared a common trade: tentmaking. Priscilla and Aquila were in Corinth because of the edict of Claudius which expelled the Jews from Rome around AD 53. There is no evidence that these two were Christians at the time they met Paul. They were more likely to have been converted while Paul lived with them and shared the gospel with them.

Every Sabbath Paul preached in the synagogue, doing his best to persuade his listeners of Jesus Christ. Paul's tentmaking work supported his ministry. However, when Silas and Timothy showed up, they arrived with a collection from the congregation at Macedonia and Paul was freed up to give himself more fully to the ministry.

Paul preached to the Jews that Jesus was the Christ but they were resistant to the Spirit (Acts 18:6). Paul threw up his hands saying, "Your blood be upon your own heads; I am clean; from henceforth I will go unto the Gentiles" (Acts 18:6 KJV), and moved forward. He went to Justus's house, whose "house joined hard to the synagogue" (Acts 18:7 KJV).

Paul discovered that all was not lost for to his surprise, Crispus, the chief ruler of the synagogue, "believed on the Lord with all his house, and many of

the Corinthians hearing believed, and were baptized"
(Acts 18:8 KJV). The Spirit was moving, and the
movement of the church continued.

In Acts 18, the Holy Spirit is seen giving Paul
assurance and the ability to withstand false accusations.
The Spirit carried him as he left dear friends, and poured
out wisdom and boldness to lovingly correct others when
they innocently taught doctrine that was not quite
accurate.

Assurance

The Holy Spirit brings assurance to those who are
witnesses for Him. One night, God spoke to Paul in a
vision, saying, "Keep it up, and don't let anyone
intimidate or silence you. No matter what happens, I'm
with you and no one is going to be able to hurt you. You
have no idea how many people I have on my side in this
city" (Acts 18:9–10 MSG). This could mean that many
would be saved in that city not had not yet converted.

This promise of the Lord did not mean Paul would not
be assaulted for preaching the message of the gospel, but
that those against him would be unsuccessful in their
efforts to stop his preaching. Paul stayed for another year
and six months (Acts 18:11). The Holy Spirit encouraged
Paul not to give up!

Accusations

The Holy Spirit also encouraged Paul to withstand
spiteful accusations. Paul was brought to Gallio, the

deputy of the province of Achaia, and accused him of trying to stir up the people with illegal worship and false religion (Acts 18:13). Before Paul had a chance to defend himself, Gallio interrupted and declared:

> *If it were a matter of wrong or wicked lewdness, O ye Jews, reason would that I should bear with you: But if it be a question of words and names, and of your law, look ye to it; for I will be no judge of such matters. And he drave them from the judgment seat.* — *Acts 18:14–16 (KJV)*

Gallio threw Paul's case out. Sosthenes, the chief ruler of the synagogue (Acts 18:17) who had replaced Crispus (and likely became a Christian as well) was accused as was Paul, and was beat up—but Gallio "cared for none of those things" (Acts 18:17 KJV).

Farewells

Paul finally left Corinth for Syria, in the confidence of the Holy Spirit who had worked among the Corinthians. He took Priscilla and Aquila with him.

Paul, Aquila, and Priscilla landed in Ephesus. Aquila and his wife stayed, but Paul left the ship briefly to go to the synagogue and preach to the Jews who wanted him to stay longer. After saying good-bye, he promised with confidence, "I'll be back, God willing" (Acts 18:21 MSG). Paul went through various cities, not to stay, but to check on the welfare of church plants.

The Spirit carried Paul's friends and new believers as they continued witnessing after Paul left.

Christ-like Corrections

Finally, Acts 18 describes a man named Apollos who came to Ephesus. He was a Jew, a good preacher—and "mighty in the scriptures" (Acts 18:24 KJV). However, Apollos only preached up to the baptism of John. Priscilla and Aquila took him aside to share with him the rest of the story, and his ministry grew.

Through Paul's time in Corinth, the Holy Spirit affirmed Paul through commonality (as Paul, Aquila and Priscilla shared in their tentmaking profession). He assured Paul in chaotic times, and assists Aquila and Priscilla as new believers in lovingly correcting others.

So, too, will the Holy Spirit affirm you when you face conflict, and assist you when you are compelled to correct someone who has erred in the Scriptures. You do not have to go about ministry alone!

CHAPTER NINETEEN

Victorious over the Occult

Acts 19

Some Jews who went around driving out evil spirits tried to invoke the name of the Lord Jesus over those who were demon-possessed. They would say, "In the name of the Jesus whom Paul preaches, I command you to come out." Seven sons of Sceva, a Jewish chief priest, were doing this. One day the evil spirit answered them, "Jesus I know, and Paul I know about, but who are you?" Then the man who had the evil spirit jumped on them and overpowered them all. He gave them such a beating that they ran out of the house naked and bleeding. — Acts 19:13–16 (NIV)

The church continued to grow as God's apostles stepped out in faith each day by the Spirit's leading. It was a movement never before seen, and had now spread to what is today Europe and Greece. Each time God's vessels of blessing faced opposition, the apostles experienced the Holy Spirit moving, intervening, and removing obstacles, which emboldened them to keep going. Because of this, their faith was strengthened and nothing phased them.

But there was another opposition that Luke addressed in Acts 19—the power of darkness. The Holy Spirit is not unaware of the evil that exists in the world we cannot see, and actually exposes the power of darkness and reigns victorious. Satan uses deception to distort and distance people from God's truths through things like sorcery, witchcraft, astrology, fortunetellers—even among Christians. New Age Spirituality popularizes all of these things.

In Acts 19, idol worship and witchcraft were prevalent in Ephesus as a normal practice. However, when the Ephesians heard the gospel they responded by doing away with all kinds of witchcraft and sorcery.

The Baptism

Paul came upon some disciples in Ephesus and discovered they had not received the Holy Spirit. Paul had asked, "Have ye received the Holy Ghost since ye believed?" And they said unto him, "We have not so much as heard whether there be any Holy Ghost" (Acts 19:2 KJV). They had only been baptized unto repentance by John. Paul explained that John preached the baptism of repentance so that people could radically change their lives to be ready to receive Jesus. Hearing this, the Ephesian disciples were baptized again in the name of Jesus.

This is the only place in the New Testament where anyone was re-baptized. John's baptism was anticipatory of Christ, and the baptism of Christ was the fulfillment of that anticipation. Paul laid hands on the disciples, and "the Holy Ghost came on them; and they spake with tongues, and prophesied" (Acts 19:6 KJV). According to Acts 19:7, about twelve men were saved that day.

The Teaching

Paul taught in Ephesus in the synagogue for three months (Acts 19:8). Resistance surfaced again from some of the listeners, "as some of them began spreading evil rumors through the congregation about the Christian way of life" (Acts 19:9 MSG). So, Paul took disciples with him and set up shop in Tyrannus's school and taught them daily about Jesus Christ for two years (Acts 18:10). Paul took enough time preaching about Jesus in the province of Asia so that both Jews and Greeks had the opportunity to hear the gospel message

The Extraordinary Miracles

The Holy Spirit poured out through Paul through extraordinary miracles. The word began to spread that people were taking pieces of clothing that had touched Paul's skin, and the pieces of the fabric had power to heal (Acts 19:12). These were uncommon miracles that helped to establish the foundation of the apostle's work, and continued to validate the gospel message.

The Counterfeits

Paul's work escalated when some traveling Jewish (occult) exorcists tried to cast out demons using the name of Jesus preached by Paul (Acts 19:13). They thought Paul had performed a magical trick. They pronounced the name of the Master Jesus over victims of evil spirits, saying, "I command you by the Jesus preached by Paul!" (Acts 19:13 MSG).

These exorcists were the seven sons of a certain Jewish high priest named Sceva. When the seven sons tried to perform an exorcist on a man, the evil spirit spoke back and said, "Jesus I know, and Paul I know; but who are ye?" (Acts 19:15 KJV).

This one sentence demands a little interpretative digging. The first use of 'know' is the word *ginōskō*, which means "to come know, understand, perceive or have knowledge of."[49] It suggests knowing someone through experience. The second use of 'know' is a different Greek word, which indicates familiar or intimate knowledge of someone[50]

The evil spirit thus said, "I know Jesus because I've experienced and interacted with Him. I am acquainted with Paul. But I do not know you (referencing Sceva's seven sons" (Acts 19:15).

The possessed man jumped on the seven sons and beat them, until they "fled out of that house naked and wounded" (Acts 19:16 KJV). Demons can sometimes cause those they possess to have unusual strength (Mark 5:3–4).

Cults and the Occult

Cults and the occult are weapons of mass deception used by Satan. Cults are religious groups or communities that are predicted by the Bible:

> But there were false prophets also among the people, even as there shall be false teachers among you, who privily shall bring in damnable heresies, even denying the Lord that bought them, and bring upon themselves swift destruction. And many shall follow their pernicious ways; by reason of whom the way of truth shall be evil spoken of.
> — *2 Peter 2:1–2 (KJV)*

Cults deviate from the foundational and historical truths of the Bible and God's revelation in Jesus Christ. Some cults try to imitate the Christian church but complicate Scripture and deny certain biblical truths such as the deity of Jesus Christ or the triune God, or they may try to add some additional readings to the Bible. Some cults are offshoots from pagan religions. The members are in bondage to the cult leader and are often under fear of leaving the cult and losing their salvation.

The occult, on the other hand, refers to what is hidden, concealed, or secret. The occult involves the spirit world of darkness not light. The occult is particularly deceptive because the spirit world is very real. People that embrace the occult are dealing with the spirit world but the source of the spirit is evil.

There are serious problems and concerns for those who dabble in cults or the occult. First, only God can read the minds of men according to 1 Corinthians 2:11:

> *For what man knoweth the things of a man, save the spirit of man which is in him? even so the things of God knoweth no man, but the Spirit of God.* *(KJV)*

Next, only God can predict the future:

> *Why, you do not even know what will happen tomorrow.*
> *— James 4:14 (NIV)*

Witchcraft, sorcery, and mediums attempt to do these things that only God can do—know man's thoughts, know the future, and perform false miracles. For this reason, participating in these things is forbidden by God (see Deuteronomy 18:9–14; Leviticus 19:31; Leviticus 20:6, 27).

Entertaining these activities is devastating for both the Christian and the church, because it sets one up to take a position that is reserved for God alone. When Paul proclaimed the gospel in Acts 19 and it was received, the liberated people gladly burned all their occult materials.

The Conversion

Return to Acts 19. Word spread that there was a new respect for God and His preacher Paul. Many gave up sorcery and burned all of their witchcraft books, valued at fifty thousand drachmas (the monetary system in Greece Acts 19:19). The Word of Jesus Christ evidently prevailed sovereign in Ephesus. Acts 19:20 says, "In this way the word of the Lord spread widely and grew in power" (NIV). In spite of the pervasive influence of evil over a city, the church movement continued to grow.

The Consequences

Paul decided it was time to move on to Macedonia and the Achaia provinces, and to Jerusalem. He had great ambitions to see Rome. He sent Timothy and Erastus ahead of him to settle things in Asia. Before Paul's departure another rebellion arose from gentiles against those who were in "the Way" (Acts 19:23 NIV).

Demetrius was the silversmith who made the silver goddess of Artemis (fertility) and as the gospel spread and people burned their shrines and idols. Demetrius's business was impacted because of Paul. He started a coup to overthrow Paul, sending the whole city in uproar (Acts 19:24). They seized two of Paul's Macedonian associates, Gaius and Aristarcus (Acts 19:29). Paul wanted to go defend the gospel and take on his opponents but the disciples and some of the officials would not let him. The Jews tried to push Alexander to take control; different factions arose to get Alexander to see their point of view.

When he opened his mouth, they realized he was a Jew, and "they all shouted in unison for about two hours: 'Great is Artemis of the Ephesians!'" (Acts 19:34 NIV).

The Conclusion

The town clerk quieted them down and said that Demetrius's argument was over man-made gods. He said Artemis was not a man-made god but rather her stone image "fell from heaven" (Acts 19:35 NIV). He commanded them to conduct themselves in a manner that was worthy of Artemis. He said Paul's men had done nothing to harm the temple or goddess. He further stated that if Demetrius and his workers had a complaint they would have to take it to court where they could accuse all they wanted. They were advised to take all complaints to the town meetings and where they would be settled; there was no excuse for the mêlée. Their behavior would bring an offense to Rome. He town clerk sent them home and Paul was cleared of any charges.

Today, the occult is increasingly accepted; sorcery, witchcraft, astrology, fortunetellers, psychics, and so forth are commonly sought after, even among Christians. New Age Spirituality popularizes all of these things. Believers must be on guard against books, music, movies, and even so-called holidays that are rooted in the power of darkness.

When cultic practices sneak in to the church, the consequences can be literally deadly and certainly destructive. But the Holy Spirit is victorious over evil spirits for those who trust Jesus and depend on God's leading.

CHAPTER TWENTY

Empowering the Saints to Completion

Acts 20

And now, behold, I go bound in the spirit unto Jerusalem, not knowing the things that shall befall me there:

Save that the Holy Ghost witnesseth in every city, saying that bonds and afflictions abide me.

But none of these things move me, neither count I my life dear unto myself, so that I might finish my course with joy, and the ministry, which I have received of the Lord Jesus, to testify the gospel of the grace of God.

— Acts 20:22–24 (KJV)

One of the most profound gifts the Holy Spirit gives the church is grace for the long haul. When it doesn't seem you can go on another day, when the finish line seems too far off and the mountains too hard to climb,

God enables believers through the power of the Holy Spirit to press on that they might leave lasting impressions for future generations.

One day, life on earth will be but a memory. Paul understood the importance of leaving a good impression—of being a model to other believers of standing firm to the end and completing the race set before him. When God's people embrace this calling, committed to following Him to the end, entire generations are impacted.

Ephesus was in an uproar because of the spread of the gospel. People's new-found faith resulted in the abandoning of superstitious beliefs. Those who stood to profit from their bondage incited a riot.

Now, in Acts 20, things had settled down in Ephesus and Paul continued to encourage the saints to continue the work. Paul left for Macedonia and ended up in Greece for three months and discovered there was a plot to kill him (Act 20:3). The Jews were waiting for Paul so he changed his travel route. He wanted to be in Jerusalem for the Feast of Unleavened bread (Passover).

Six men accompanied him into Asia Sopater of Berea included Aristarchus, Secundus, Gaius, Timotheus, Tychicus and Trophimus; three were from Macedonia and three were from Asia Minor. They carried with them funds (the collection for the poor saints at Rome) and met in Troas.

Acts 20:7 is the clearest verse in the New Testament that the normal meeting day of the apostolic church was Sunday. The Scriptures do not indicate what time Paul began his sermon but he preached past midnight. It was late and no doubt some were beginning to grow sleepy as evident in Acts 20:2–10:

And there sat in a window a certain young man named Eutychus, being fallen into a deep sleep: and as Paul was long preaching, he sunk down with sleep, and fell down from the third loft, and was taken up dead. And Paul went down, and fell on him, and embracing him said, Trouble not yourselves; for his life is in him. — **Acts 20:9–10 (KJV)**

As Paul preached, a young man named Eutychus had fallen from a third story window and died. Paul embraced Eutychus and the young man came alive. They then participated in the Lord's Supper and fellowshipped until morning. Paul stayed in Troas longer than he anticipated so he sent others on ahead of him. He avoided a stop in Ephesus because he wanted to arrive in Jerusalem by the day of Pentecost.

After this short story about Eutychus, Acts 20 introduces Paul's farewell sermon, broken into four parts: his past, his present, and his future, and their responsibility.

His Past

Paul reminded the church how he sacrificed his life for the furtherance of the gospel. In the face of constant opposition he didn't quit. In Acts 20:20 Paul said, "I kept back nothing that was profitable unto you." He gave them every truth and encouragement he could to impact their lives. He had a proven track record of trying to persuade people to live for Jesus Christ.

His Present

Paul then declared the condition of the present church—and that the Holy Spirit had pressed him to go to Jerusalem. He did not know what was ahead (Act 20:22). The Holy Spirit warned him hard times and imprisonment were awaiting him, as he surmised, "bonds and afflictions abide me" (Acts 20:23). Paul was at a point in his ministry where he was able to say that "none of these things move me, neither count I my life dear unto myself, so that I might finish my course with joy, and the ministry, which I have received of the Lord Jesus, to testify the gospel of the grace of God" (Acts 20:24). The only thing that mattered to Paul was telling others about the good news of the grace of God. Paul gave the church his final good-bye and placed emphasis on the fact that they would "see my face no more" (Acts 20:25).

Paul's Future and the Church's Responsibility

Paul warned the church that as soon as he was gone attacks would afflict the body; "grievous wolves [shall] enter in among you, not sparing the flock" (Acts 20:29).

He told them leaders were responsible for guarding and defending the faith of the church that Jesus purchased with His own blood. Paul reminded them that for three years he had tried to warn them—with tears

(Act 20:31). He wanted to guard the truth so much that he was moved with compassion when he thought about false doctrine being taught.

Now the responsibility was in the their hands; Paul commended them to the grace of God (Acts 20:32). He was confident that God's grace would do for them what it had done for him. God's grace is to "build you up, and to give you an inheritance among all them which are sanctified" (Acts 20:32). He tried to demonstrate the importance of working on behalf of the weak and not exploiting them, and then he gave them a final parting word of wisdom: "It is more blessed to give than to receive" (Act 20:35).

Paul dropped to his knees, his brothers and sisters in Christ kneeling with him, and prayed. With tears his church family bravely walked him down to the ship for departure.

There is always something sentimental about departures: the shedding of tears, the embracing of bodies, and the words that are shared. Paul left a lasting impression on the saints in Ephesus and he gave a strong farewell speech that left them encouraged. Paul experienced His fate.

Unexpected issues will arise with to you, too. But don't be afraid—God has already ordained each day. Learn from Paul, the example of one who allowed the Holy Spirit to direct his life and order his days. When Paul was discouraged, He encouraged others. When obstacles crept in, he allowed the Holy Spirit to re-direct his path. God gave him the grace to endure his foes, and the ability to embrace his future. Though he didn't know what darkness was ahead, what mattered most to him was finishing the work started. What a model for all believers, called to be witnesses to the world!

CHAPTER TWENTY-ONE

The Sustainer of Ministry

Acts 21

And all the city was moved, and the people ran together: and they took Paul, and drew him out of the temple: and forthwith the doors were shut. And as they went about to kill him, tidings came unto the chief captain of the band, that all Jerusalem was in an uproar. — Acts 21:30–31 (KJV)

Faithfulness in ministry often leads to being misunderstood, but the Holy Spirit gives information, confirmation and determination to go forward. Paul experienced this during the third part of his missionary journey. However, the Holy Spirit continues to affirm and confirm that what was happening to him was for a purpose: for the testimony of the gospel of Jesus.

Set for Jerusalem

In the first verses of Acts 21, the apostle had sailed through various ports for three days. Paul and his companions had found a boat going directly to Phoenicia and voyaged about four hundred miles to a city named Tyre where they met other believers.

There was no synagogue in Tyre. It took the ship a week to unload and load cargo and Paul stayed with the believers for seven days. Their message to Paul was that "he should not go up to Jerusalem" (Acts 21:4 KJV). When it was time to leave the believers they tearfully bid Paul farewell—though they had only known him for a week.

When they reached Ptolemais, they met friends whom they stayed with for a day. In the morning, they went to Caesarea, found Philip and stayed with him that day along with his four daughters who prophesied. After a few days, a prophet named Agabus arrived who went straight to Paul, took his belt and tied himself up and said, "The Holy Spirit says, 'In this way the Jewish leaders in Jerusalem will bind the owner of this belt and will hand him over to the Gentiles'" (Acts 21:11 NIV).

When the people heard this, they begged Paul not to go. Then, in Acts 21:12, Paul told the people to stop all the dramatics because they misunderstood his mission. The issue was not what would happen to him, but what God would accomplish through his obedience to the ministry he had been called to. His mission was to sacrifice his life for the testimony of the gospel.

The people gave up trying to convince Paul and after a few days Paul and his companions were on their way to Jerusalem. Some of the believers in Caesarea accompanied Paul and took him by the home of "Mnason of Cyprus, and old disciple" (Acts 21:16 KJV), who invited him to lodge there overnight.

Paul's Message Was Misunderstood by the Church

Paul finally arrived in Jerusalem and met with James and other leaders of the church and delivered the offering to the church leaders. Paul told them what the Lord had done concerning the gentiles through his ministry. They gave God the praise but they had a story to tell as well.

The Jews were not really happy with Paul's presence in Jerusalem. Jews were becoming believers, but they were trying to bring the law of Moses with their new-found faith. The Jewish converts were zealots that had been fed misleading information that Paul was advising believing Jews to do away with the law of Moses and circumcision.

James and others in church leadership were not happy. They misunderstood Paul's message and looked at him as an unguided missile bringing unnecessary attention to the church. The leaders had said when the Jews found out Paul was in town there was "bound to be trouble" (Acts 21:22). So, the church came up with a plan for Paul to win the disgruntled Jewish believers over and settle rumors.

Four men were to pay a vow but did not have the money. The leaders suggested Paul pay their vow and join them in the vow ceremony to put the rumors to rest. They assured Paul that they had not backslid on the previous arrangement in Acts 15, so Paul did as they requested.

Paul's Ministry Was Misunderstood by the Jews

A group of Jews recognized Paul in the temple and a riotous scene ensued. They grabbed Paul and incited the crowd. The trouble makers claimed Paul defiled them and lied about their religion and the temple, and that Paul had brought Greeks into the temple. They said this because they saw Paul walking with a Greek and assumed that he had taken the man to the temple.

Paul was dragged outside the temple gates which were quickly locked so he could not get back in the temple. They beat him and tried to kill him. Word got back to the captain of the guard that Jerusalem was in an uproar (Acts 21:31); the people were trying to kill Paul and only stopped beating Him when they saw the chief captain with his soldiers approaching (Acts 21:32). The captain of the guard had Paul detained. He tried to question Paul but the crowd was too loud. He had Paul taken into the barracks when Paul turned to the captain and said, "May I speak unto thee" (Acts 21:37 KJV). The captain was surprised Paul spoke in Greek. The captain was surprised because he thought Paul to be an Egyptian that had been the center of controversy some time before (Acts 21:38). Paul told him who he was and asked could he address the crowd to clear up any misunderstandings. The captain gave him license, so "Paul stood on the stairs, and beckoned with the hand unto the people. And when there was made a great silence, he spake unto them in the Hebrew tongue" (Acts 21:40 KJV).

Miraculously, the Holy Spirit sustained Paul's ministry when its messenger was misunderstood. He will do the same for believers today. First, the Holy Spirit will affirm information concerning your purpose. In Acts 20, the Holy Spirit

affirmed what would be up ahead for Paul—suffering was awaiting him in Jerusalem. Then in Acts 21, the Holy Spirit confirmed Paul's suffering was for a purpose—for the testimony of the gospel. Since this was Paul's life purpose, it brought comfort.

In the same way, believers today who walk closely with the Spirit will know what is ahead—when they are grounded in the Word of God. They may experience suffering for a while, but not without purpose. 1 Peter 5:10 says, "And after you have suffered a little while, the God of all grace, who has called you to his eternal glory in Christ, will himself restore, confirm, strengthen, and establish you" (ESV). The Spirit uses suffering to restore, confirm, strengthen and establish.

CHAPTER TWENTY-TWO

The Power of Personal Testimonies

Acts 22

*Men, brethren, and fathers, hear ye my defence which I
make now unto you. (And when they heard that he spake in
the Hebrew tongue to them, they kept the more silence: and
he saith,) I am verily a man which am a Jew, born in
Tarsus, a city in Cilicia, yet brought up in this city at the
feet of Gamaliel, and taught according to the perfect
manner of the law of the fathers, and was zealous toward
God, as ye all are this day. —Acts 22:1–3 (KJV)*

When the Holy Spirit changes a person's life, a
testimony is established. It is personal and one-of-a-kind,
and no one can argue the testimony is true because it is
their story.

It is the testimony of the saints that gives meaning
behind the gospel. When a person accepts Jesus and
crosses from death to life, they are transformed. They are

a new creation (2 Corinthians 5:17). This is their testimony!

There is an interesting verse in Revelation 12:11 regarding the power of the testimony. The apostle John wrote within the context of God's coming Kingdom and the defeat of the enemy, "And *they* (the saints) have conquered *him* (the enemy) by the blood of the Lamb and by the word of their testimony, for they loved not their lives even unto death" (ESV, emphasis added).

This was the exclamation point on Paul's life, and should be the focus of every believer who is committed to the movement of the church. Followers of Jesus have a testimony that Revelation 12:11 says conquers the enemy.

Every Christian has a testimony, but they also have a responsibility to speak their story.

The Greatest Story

In the previous chapter, Paul found himself in another bind. After he had been beaten in the temple he asked the chief captain for permission to speak to the crowd. At the end of Acts 21, Paul had started speaking in the Hebrew language to clear up some misunderstandings. He did not want to miss the opportunity to capture the crowd's attention, and he knew that Jews in the courtyard would be impressed when he spoke the old Israelite language.

By doing so, he immediately identified his Jewish historicity. The crowd knew his association with Gamaliel, so they listened more attentively. Because

Gamaliel was highly respected among the Jews, Paul gained a bit of respect by being Gamaliel's student.

With the Holy Spirit undergirding him, Paul gave his testimony in three parts—focusing first on his past, then on his conversion, and finally on his new life as a believer. This is a model for believers today—an effective way to organize your story when sharing it with others.

The Criminal

Paul first relayed his past as what he was as a criminal—a man whose main goal was to seek out and imprison and kill Jews who claimed belief in Jesus as Messiah. He shared who he was in his past life, who he was before the Holy Spirit took over residence in his soul and transformed him to a person who now loved followers of Jesus.

Paul confessed, "I persecuted this way unto the death, binding and delivering into prisons both men and women. As also the high priest doth bear me witness, and all the estate of the elders: from whom also I received letters unto the brethren, and went to Damascus, to bring them which were there bound unto Jerusalem, for to be punished" (Acts 22:4–5 KJV).

The Conversion

Paul next declared what happened that change his life:

And it came to pass, that, as I made my journey, and was come nigh unto Damascus about noon, suddenly there shone from heaven a great light round about me. And I fell unto the ground, and heard a voice saying unto me, Saul, Saul, why persecutest thou me? And I answered, Who art thou, Lord? And he said unto me, I am Jesus of Nazareth, whom thou persecutest. — Acts 22:6–8 (KJV)

Paul tells of his conversion experience when he encountered Jesus. The One he had been persecuting— Jesus—revealed Himself to Paul in a powerful way and from that moment on, He knew Jesus was the Messiah. He was a transformed Jewish man, whose entire life would focus on sharing this good news with the world— both Jews and gentiles.

The Christian

Finally, Paul proclaimed who he was in the present. In Acts 22:11–21 Paul received and responded to his assignment.

Paul acknowledged that Christ sent him forward to the gentiles and that Jerusalem was not his place for ministry (Acts 22:21). His field was the world, and his mission was to spread the gospel to the Greek and to the Barbarians, to the Romans, and to the world for God had said, "for I will send thee far hence unto the Gentiles" (Acts 22:21 KJV). Paul informed the crowd that the people they despised were to be included as the sheep of God.

As soon as Paul mentioned the gentiles, the crowd went completely hostile. They began to yell and scream that Paul was a man not fit to live. He then told the crowd that Jesus, whom they crucified, was the Messiah.

For his words, Paul was called a traitor. The crowd violently expressed their dissent by casting off their clothes and throwing dust in the air. The tribune did not understand Aramaic and was confused of what was going on, so he decided to beat it out of Paul. In Acts 22:24, the chief captain ordered Paul be scourged, or whipped, in hopes of forcing him to change his speech.

Instead, this is where Paul played his last card. He affirmed he was a Roman citizen. To bind a Roman citizen was a serious offense, but scourging a Roman was illegal. To do either without a trial was the most serious offense. The centurion then rushed to make the tribune aware of Paul's Roman status. The Emperor Claudius made Roman citizenship available to anyone for a large cash payment, and misunderstanding what Paul was saying, was surprised because they could not fathom such a poor Jew could have such finance.

However, Paul announced, "I was free born" (Acts 22:28 KJV). Paul did not pay for his citizenship because his father was a citizen. It is possible that Paul's family were made citizens by some great service they rendered to the Roman Empire while living in Tarsus. Some suppose that Tarsus was a Roman colony and that is how Paul obtained citizenship but there is no proof.

The next day Paul was brought down to the Sanhedrin council to see if they could make sense out of Him. He then prepared to give his testimony before "the chief priests and all their council" (Acts 22:30 KJV).

An Example for All Believers

Paul's example of his testimony is one every person who has believed in Christ can follow. A Christian testimony is just that—only a Christian can have a story of coming to faith. A Christian testimony is established based on an encounter with Jesus Christ. And thirdly, a Christian testimony involves being able to share your story by articulating what you have observed and what you have learned about Jesus Christ personally.

A Christian testimony has three components that align with Paul's in Acts 22: a painful past delinquency, a pivotal point of decision, and a persuasive, present declaration.

A Painful Past Delinquency—Criminal

This is the beginning of your testimony when you share with honesty who you were before Christ—a criminal. You were without God and without hope (Ephesians 2:12) and standing condemned under God's righteous judgment for sin. This is who you once were.

A Pivotal Point of Decision—Conversion

A Christian must have a conversion experience. A conversion experience is when your life meets a crossroad and you make the decision to follow Christ. A Christian testimony is not necessarily a physical encounter as Paul had, but it is based on a personal relationship with Jesus Christ that has changed your life.

A Persuasive Present Declaration—Christian

Most Christians cannot or will not articulate their testimony because they cannot pinpoint when they had a conversion experience. They know they are saved, but cannot put into words how it happened. What did it do? What were the results? If someone were to ask you, "Why are you a Christian?" what would you say? Would you say you were raised in church, or would you speak of your encounter with Christ? That's the real question.

Have you had an encounter with Christ that validates your Christianity? What difference has Jesus Christ made in your life? What's your story? A Christian should be able to articulate his or her testimony no matter who agrees or disagrees. Persuasion is a part of your testimony; your story should sway others to come to Jesus Christ.

The Holy Spirit establishes your personal testimony, and does so through testing.

When you were at life's crossroads and were faced with the decision to follow Christ, or not, you made a decision. You either decided to follow Jesus Christ or not. If you did, in that moment, your own personal testimony began. This is the story that will help others know Jesus Christ.

The Bible is a compilation of testimonies God has left for His people to strengthen them and help them to know Christ better. It is the testimony of the saints that gives meaning behind the gospel. And it is your testimony that will influence others to understand the gospel, too.

CHAPTER TWENTY-THREE

Courage to Stay the Course

Acts 23

And when it was day, certain of the Jews banded together, and bound themselves under a curse, saying that they would neither eat nor drink till they had killed Paul. And they were more than forty which had made this conspiracy. And they came to the chief priests and elders, and said, We have bound ourselves under a great curse, that we will eat nothing until we have slain Paul. — Acts 23:12–14 (KJV)

Paul found himself once again before the Sanhedrin (the Jewish ruling council). He had caused a dissension between the Pharisees and the Sadducees, and now the Jews planned to kill Him.

Christians will face dark times like Paul—it's inevitable. But the Holy Spirit gives the Christian courage to stand against critics and encouragement to stay the course. He often encourages and comforts with truths the believer already knows.

210 · OSCAR T. MOSES

The Disrespect

This was Paul's third day of continuous attacks. He had continued his testimony with boldness after the high priest Ananias ordered him to be slapped in the face for saying he had lived before God with a good conscience. Paul responded to the act by calling the high priest a hypocrite for judging him by the law and then slapping him, which was against the law (Acts 23:3). The Bible compares this kind of person to white washed tombs that look "beautiful on the outside but on the inside are full of the bones of the dead and everything unclean" (Matthew 23:27 NIV).

The high priest's aids chided Paul for talking to "God's high priest" in the tone he did (Acts 23:4 NIV). Paul responded in a manner that suggested that he was not aware that Ananias was the high priest.

The Division

Paul "perceived that the one part were Sadducees, and the other Pharisees" and announced that he, too, was a Pharisee (Acts 23:6 KJV). He turned the crowd on one another by bringing up the resurrection (Act 23:6), a known disagreement between the two groups. The Pharisees believed in the resurrection but the Sadducees had nothing to do with the resurrection, angels or the Spirit.

The Pharisees defended Paul and said: "We find no evil in this man: but if a spirit or an angel hath spoken to him, let us not fight against God" (Acts 23:9 KJV). The

captain feared Paul would be seized so he ordered Paul
to be taken by force and brought to the castle.

The Vision of the Lord

The following night, the Lord stood by Paul in a
vision and encouraged him, "Be of good cheer," and also
confirmed his assignment in Rome (Acts 23:11 KJV).
God encouraged Paul at the most difficult time of his life
and continued to give Paul directions for what he should
do.

Most people embrace encouragement but don't want
directives—especially when those directives will
ultimately result in death. But at the darkest point of his
life God told Paul he must bear witness of Jesus in
Rome. This was the fourth vision the Lord gave Paul (cf.
9:4-6; 16:9; 18:9-10).

The Vow of the Enemy

Certain Jews, around forty of them, bound themselves
under a curse that they would not eat or drink until they
killed Paul. They even informed the chief priest and
elders of their vow. The Greek verb used to
communicate this concept of being under a 'curse' is
anathema, which means "a thing set up or laid by in
order to be kept." It is specifically, "an offering resulting
from a vow."[51]

A person binds himself under a curse if he does not
fulfill a vow. A lawyer would have to lift a vow. The
people conjured a plan to manipulate the chief priest into

bringing Paul to them—they vowed they would not eat anything "until we have slain Paul" (Acts 23:14 KJV).

The Informant and Important Instructions

Paul's nephew heard of the Jews' plan and told Paul of this plan while he waited in prison. Paul informed the centurions that his nephew had pertinent information for the chief captain, Claudius. Paul's nephew was brought before Claudius where he exposed the plot in full. Claudius sent him on his way charging him not to tell a soul. Claudius rounded up a small army of two hundred men to go to Caesarea, seventy horsemen, and two hundred light infantry, and sent them out that night. This was the third time Paul left a city at night in this manner (Acts 23:23; see also Acts 9:25 and Acts 17:10).

The instructions were to bring Paul safely before Felix, the governor. When a prisoner was sent to a superior, the officer bringing him had to have a letter of statement concerning the case. Claudius's letter described Paul's. He twisted the truth and said that he rescued Paul because he found out Paul was a Roman citizen. He also conveniently left out the fact that he was about to have Paul beaten.

The letter became highly important in Acts 23:29 when Claudius declared Paul innocent. When they arrived with Paul, Governor Felix held a minor interrogation. When he learned Paul was from Cilicia, he decided to hear the case, but witnesses against Paul needed to be present. Paul was subsequently locked up in Herod's official quarters.

Life Lesson

Acts 23 challenges every Christian to stand firm and be courageous. What is your story? How do you handle life when crisis arise? Do you fall apart? Jesus wants those who trust Him to be encouraged; He used the phrases, "be of good courage" or "take courage" five times in the New Testament and each circumstance brought the person involved comfort. He told the sick of the palsy, "Take heart, my son, your sins are forgiven" (Matthew 9:2 ESV). He calmed His fearful disciples as He walked to them across the water in Matthew 14:27 and Mark 6:50, calling them to "take courage. It is I" (NIV). He told the woman with the issue of blood in Matthew 9:22 to "take heart" (ESV), and in the Upper Room the night of his betrayal in John 16:33 he told His disciples to "take heart" (NIV).

When confronted with issues concerning faith, believe the Holy Spirit will help. The Holy Spirit will comfort anyone who follows Jesus, and will remind them of what they already know. "Take heart" when representing Jesus Christ and finish the course.

CHAPTER TWENTY-FOUR

A Christian Character and a Clear Conscience

Acts 24

The Holy Spirit assists the Christian by giving a clear conscience and maintaining Godly character when faith is challenged.

The Christian should constantly live in self-examination and urgently embrace life application. If the Christian has a clear conscience before God he or she will be fruitful in their worship, work, witness, and the Word of God. Paul always sought to keep his conscience clear (Acts 23:1, 24:16).

In Acts 23, Felix had agreed to hear Paul's case. The text unfolds five days later with the apostle standing before Felix. The context of Acts 24 can be understood in terms of three sections or themes: absurd accusations, divine defense, and private preaching.

Absurd Accusations Against Paul

Ananias—the high priest— and the elders hired an attorney named Tertullus to present their accusations against Paul. Tertullus immediately began to accuse Paul, saying, "Seeing that by thee we enjoy great quietness, and that very worthy deeds are done unto this nation by thy providence," (Acts 24:2 KJV).

Tertullus poured out flattery over Felix full of mistruths about his character. He bestowed honorable accolades of integrity upon Felix that were not true. Felix was a corrupt leader. Tertullus then hurled absurd accusations of sedition upon Paul that were not true. In Acts 24:9, the Jews agreed with Tertullus's mistruths.

He had attacked Paul from four perspectives. First, he attacked the person of Paul: He called Paul's character into question: "this man a pestilent fellow" he lied (Acts 24:5 KJV).

He next attacked Paul's purpose, saying he was "a mover of sedition among all the Jews throughout the world" (Acts 24:5 KJV). A "mover of sedition" is one who excites turmoil, one who is disingenuous. The character and conduct of a mover of sedition don't match up.

Tertullus then attacked Paul's position of faith: "and a ringleader of the sect of the Nazarenes" (Acts 24:5 KJV). Judaism was tolerated but any new religion was considered a cult. These leaders did not associate Christianity with Judaism but viewed it as an unauthorized cult.

Finally, Tertullus accused Paul of profaning of the temple (Acts 24:6). The Roman government gave Jews permission to execute any gentile who went inside the barrier of the temple.

Satan has a way of making evil appear good and good appear evil. Christians will sometimes be accused and ostracized while immoral troublemakers within the church receive accolades and well wishes—just as Tertullus did with Paul. It is no wonder, for "Satan himself is transformed into an angel of light" (2 Corinthians 11:14 KJV).

The Divine Defense from Paul

Paul spoke truth to power! He responded to the Tertullus's accusations on point. The Jews did not know that Claudius Lysias letter substantiated all that he said. Paul maintained respect. He recognized Felix's' authority and he maintained conduct. He answered the charges levied against him by declaring his innocence. Finally, he maintained his conscience: Paul defended his actions by pointing out his motivation. He told them his motivation was to bring alms to the Jewish believers who needed assistance.

The Asian Jews would testify of his presence in the temple being orderly, but they did not inquire of the Asian Jews' presence at the hearing. The Jews were upset over doctrinal issues, and because Paul had proclaimed the resurrection of Jesus Christ from the dead.

There is no neutral ground where right and wrong is concerned. Paul was called to explain to his accusers the *cause* of his faith in Christ, yet did not fail to *reason* with them of "righteousness, temperance, and judgment to come" (Acts 24:25 KJV). Paul drew the line between right and wrong. There was no coddling.

Paul's Private Preaching

Deferring the case was the easy way out for Felix. He possessed Lysias's letter that condemned the Jewish leaders. He wanted to keep peace with the Jews but he also loved money and wanted a bribe from Paul for his release. He detained Paul under the pretense that he had to await Lysias's testimony.

The more important issue in this section was the meeting between Felix, his wife Drusilla, and Paul. In this meeting, Paul preached Jesus Christ to the couple:

> And as he reasoned of righteousness, temperance, and judgment to come, Felix trembled, and answered, Go thy way for this time; when I have a convenient season, I will call for thee. — *Acts 24:25 (KJV)*

The tables had turned. Paul was no longer on trial, but instead Felix was on trial before Paul. Paul could refute the charges made against him but Felix could not refute the sin charges Paul had charged to Felix, who trembled and said he would call for Paul at "a convenient season."

Felix put off his opportunity to come to Jesus Christ. The season for getting right with God is when His Word pricks a person's heart and when they tremble under the power of His Word. The writer of Proverbs said, "Boast not thyself of to morrow; for thou knowest not what a day may bring forth" (Proverbs 27:1 KJV). Don't put off tomorrow what can be done today.

The lesson is a clinical case study the blessing of living a life of good conscience before God. If the Christian has a clear conscience before God he or she will be fruitful in their worship, work, witness, and the Word of God.

Paul had always sought to keep his conscience clear; when trials arose, his character remained and his life continued to be a reflection of Christ in spite of false charges. When the church maintains godly character, it speaks without words. People watch are drawn to God.

THE MOVEMENT IN ACTS · 221

The Provider of Patience

Acts 25

> *Now when Festus was come into the province, after three days he ascended from Caesarea to Jerusalem. Then the high priest and the chief of the Jews informed him against Paul, and besought him, and desired favour against him, that he would send for him to Jerusalem, laying wait in the way to kill him.* — *Acts 25:1–3 (KJV)*

Sometimes hardships are part of the journey to get to intended destinations. When there is nothing that can be done, and it seems time is slipping away, the Holy Spirit will provide an unexplainable ability to tolerate or accept circumstances until the difficult time passes. Patience is an attribute of Christ and as such, is something all Christians should pursue—especially in the days ahead. For the church movement to advance, believers must learn to wait.

Patience ... Please!

Patience is the capacity to accept or tolerate delay, trouble, or suffering, without becoming annoyed or upset.[52] The apostle Paul waited patiently in prison for two years. His ministry had been put on hold, the promise of God had been delayed, and constant opposition had become a way of life . There were likely moments when Paul sat in prison and asked God, "You said I would make it to Rome to preach the gospel but every turn I make is met with opposition. Did I hear You right?"

In Acts 24, Felix had sought to receive money for Paul's release from prison. As a consequence, Paul was left sitting in prison for two years. In Acts 25, Festus replaced Felix as governor at the protest of Jewish leadership. Festus was a novice, inexperienced in his new position—and the Jews knew this. In contrast, Felix was an old pro, a crooked politician of sorts. He understood the Jews, he was informed about Christianity, and he had political savvy while Festus knew nothing of Jewish affairs. He was a "green," amateur governor.

But God used the Jews obstinacy and unbelief to accomplish His plans for Paul's ministry. The Holy Spirit once again set the stage for the gospel through opposition as Paul preached the gospel. What seemed a series of slip-ups, actually paved the way for Paul to complete his assignment and preach the gospel in Rome.

The Holy Spirit developed patience in Paul over the course of his three missionary journeys; individual believers as well as the church will be refined and grown as they learn patience through similar situations.

Patience Is Developed Through Testing

James 1:2–3 says, "My brethren, count it all joy when ye fall into divers temptations; Knowing this, that the trying of your faith worketh patience" (KJV). Trials and temptations work out patience in a person in a way nothing else can. When difficulties arise and there is nothing you can do to "fix" a situation, the only thing you *can* do is trust the Holy Spirit for His patience to work itself out in you.

Patience Is Developed Through Waiting

Psalm 37:7 says, "Rest in the LORD, and wait patiently for him: fret not thyself because of him who prospereth in his way, because of the man who bringeth wicked devices to pass" (KJV). Galatians 6:9 says, "And let us not be weary in well doing: for in due season we shall reap, if we faint not" (KJV). Waiting for anything forces people to respond one of two ways: impatiently (agitated, irritated, and watching the clock) or in trust and peace knowing God's timing is perfect. Patience is perfectly developed through waiting.

Patience Is Developed by Standing on God's Promises

Paul said in 2 Corinthians 1:20, "For all the promises of God in him are yea, and in him Amen, unto the glory of God by us" (KJV). God's promises never change, and everything He says will happen will come to pass. Standing firm on these promises further develops the ability to relax and wait.

Patience Is Developed Through Prayer

Luke 18:1 says, "And he spake a parable unto them to this end, that men ought always to pray, and not to faint" (KJV). When struggling with patience, seek the One who is not bound by time to help you develop a spirit that trusts in God's understanding of time.

Patience Is Developed by Remembering God's Sovereignty

The prophet Isaiah wrote, "For my thoughts are not your thoughts, neither are your ways my ways, saith the LORD" (Isaiah 55:8 KJV). Sometimes it might seem like God is not showing up soon enough, or dealing with sin quickly enough. Promises He made may not have come to pass, and it may be difficult to believe they ever will. Remember God's sovereignty over all things—and that His ways are far above man's. This, too, will re-focus you on allowing God's timing to play out.

Patience Is Developed Through Anticipating God's Direction

Proverbs 3:5–6 reminds God's people to "Trust in the LORD with all thine heart; and lean not unto thine own understanding. In all thy ways acknowledge him, and he shall direct thy paths" (KJV). God promises to direct believers' paths. Trust Him for what you cannot yet see.

Paul learned to trust in the Holy Spirit for patience while He waited for God's promise to him to come to fruition.

The Aggravation

The governor, Felix, was replaced by Festus and the Jewish high priest pursued him. For two years no action had been taken against Paul but when Festus took office the Jews sought to reopen Paul's case. Festus wanted to make a good impression on the Jews but he knew very little about Jewish matters.

The Jews attempted to trick Festus into sending Paul to Jerusalem so they could assassinate him, but Festus answered that Paul should remain in Caesarea (Acts 25:3). Festus met with them some time after and had Paul brought before them. When Paul came forth the Jews levied unproven charges against him. In Acts 25:8, Paul defended all the charges before him. However, Festus wanted to please the Jews and asked Paul if he would go to Jerusalem; Paul declined and chided Festus. Paul sensed a trap in Acts 25:9, and did not go along with the Jerusalem plan. He knew the trip would have been dangerous, and also remembered the forty Jews from two years prior who had made a vow to kill him.

There was no chance Paul would receive a fair trial in Jerusalem. Paul saw justice taking a back seat to politics and convenience. Finally, Paul was able to make his appeal to Rome:

> *I stand at Caesar's judgment seat, where I ought to be judged: to the Jews have I done no wrong, as thou very well knowest. For if I be an offender, or have committed any thing worthy of death, I refuse not to die: but if there be none of these things whereof these accuse me, no man may deliver me unto them. I appeal unto Caesar. Then Festus, when he had conferred with the council, answered, Hast thou appealed unto Caesar? unto Caesar shalt thou go.* — *Acts 25:10–12 (KJV)*

The Jews knew Paul had not done anything wrong—certainly nothing worthy of death. And still he would be investigated.

The Investigation

Agrippa and Bernice came to Caesarea to salute Festus. Festus explained Paul's case to Agrippa. Festus was the procurator and Rome's area representative but Agrippa was well versed in Jewish law and matters. Festus needed help and Agrippa agreed to hear the case because he wanted to know more about Christianity.

The next day Agrippa and Bernice entered the courtroom with pomp and a host of dignitaries with them. Festus confessed that Paul was innocent. However, Festus had a serious problem: if he released Paul the Jews would surely riot. If he handed Paul over, he would have been handing a Roman citizen over to be lynched. The case was out of his hands; he had no other choice but to hand it to Augustus' court. He wanted Agrippa to examine Paul so he could know what to write in his report, saying, "Wherefore I have brought him forth before you, and specially before thee, O king Agrippa, that, after examination had, I might have somewhat to write" (Acts 25:26 KJV).

The Holy Spirit prepared Paul with patience while in prison but at the same time prepared the platform for Paul to share the gospel in the next chapter, Acts 26. Patience is an attribute of Christ that all Christians must pursue. Regardless of whether circumstances are good and peaceful or hard and trying, God calls believers to trust him by enduring patiently and remembering God is in control.

CHAPTER TWENTY-SIX

Creating Consistent Lives

Acts 26

Paul is clear, confident, and consistent in his testimony. If you desire to do anything great for God, you must be consistent. Consistently examine your commitment, exercise good conduct, and express your convictions

The word 'consistent' means "marked by harmony, regularity, or steady continuity." It also means "showing steady conformity to character."[53]

Being consistent can have positive and negative associations. Positive connotations would include former Chicago Bulls star Michael Jordan and his ability to consistently score in clutch game situations or the ability of Perry Mason to consistently win case after case. Negative connotations could refer to consistent crime in African American communities that seems to soar each year or being consistently late for work. Sometimes consistency could be referred to how often one is *inconsistent*. Some people can be consistent with inconsistency.

His Conduct in Controversy

In Acts 26, Paul taught how vitally important it is for the Christian to be consistent. Paul was consistent with the gospel message of Jesus Christ.

While in chains, Paul gave his final defense for the case of the resurrected Jesus in an attempt to convert unbelievers to the Christian faith. In this chapter, Paul was about to make his defense to Festus. When Agrippa gave Paul the floor to speak, the first thing he said was, "King Agrippa, I consider myself fortunate to stand before you today as I make my defense against all the accusations of the Jews" (Acts 26:2 NIV). His remained consistent with how it had been through many other trials, tribulations, and celebrations. Whatever situation he found himself in, he always looked for the silver lining.

His Communication of Christ

Paul also consistently shared his testimony of Jesus Christ and the difference Christ had made in his life. In Acts 26:4, Paul shared his testimony *again*, to King Agrippa. This was the third time in the book of Acts that Paul gave the same testimony. It did not change! It's the same story, but Paul's passion for Christ caused him to tell the story each time as though it was the first time.

His Commitment to His Conviction

In Acts 19, Paul explained his assignment from God was to obey and remain committed to what God had called him to do. He said, "But God has helped me to this very day; so I stand here and testify to small and great alike" (Acts 26:22). He declared how he had continued to witness to both small and great about Jesus Christ.

After Agrippa and Festus listened patiently to Paul's testimony, Festus called him crazy. "You are out of your mind, Paul!" he shouted. "Your great learning is driving you insane" (Acts 26:24). Paul stood his ground and said, "I am not insane, most excellent Festus. What I am saying is true and reasonable" (Acts 25:25). King Agrippa knew exactly what Paul was talking about because none of what Paul said was hidden from him.

Paul turned to Agrippa and asked him straight forward, "do you believe the prophets? I know you do" (Act 26:27 NIV). This was yet another example of Paul's consistent commitment. He never missed the opportunity to make an appeal for Christ.

Agrippa was trapped in a corner, and his only way of escape was to flip the script with the statement he makes in Acts 26:28: "Almost thou persuadest me to be a Christian." The NIV translation suggests that Agrippa asked a question instead of providing a statement: "Do you think that in such a short time you can persuade me to be a Christian?" (Acts 26:28 NIV).

The Greek translation says, "In such a short time are you trying to convert me?" Whether it was a statement or a question the context still remains the same. "Almost" is just as dangerous as "not at all!" Paul remained committed to his call and said, "I pray God that not only you but all who are listening to me today may become what I am, except for these chains" (Acts 26:29 NIV).

The king arose with the governor, Bernice, and those sitting with them. They went to another room to confer about Paul's defense. They agreed that Paul had done nothing to deserve death or imprisonment. Agrippa said to Festus, "This man could have been set free if he had not appealed to Caesar" (Acts 26:32 NIV).

Paul encourages believers to be consistent in the faith. In this generation, persecution is increasing against Christians, and no one knows how much worse it might get. There may come a day when believers will have to stand up and profess what they believe—under penalty of death. No matter what, the church must remain consistent in its conduct, communication, and commitment to the call. Examine your commitment, exercise good conduct—integrity goes a long way! And express your convictions. Be ready to state with a clear conscience that you have given the Lord your best and that your relationship and duty to Christ is what truly matters.

The story is really not about you. It's about God's Kingdom and being a vital part of keeping the movement of this coming Kingdom alive.

CHAPTER TWENTY-SEVEN

Confidence for Life's Dark Storms

Acts 27

But the centurion, willing to save Paul, kept them from their purpose; and commanded that they which could swim should cast themselves first into the sea, and get to land:

And the rest, some on boards, and some on broken pieces of the ship. And so it came to pass, that they escaped all safe to land. — Acts 27:43–44 (KJV)

There are times in life where believers will face obstacles, accusations, and misunderstanding. Those are tough seasons. However, a season may come that surpasses these—a dark season of life where you think you might not make it out alive.

When the storms of life come (and they will), Christians must have confidence in an internal anchor— the Lord alone. The Lord will help His children make it through the dark night. Proverbs 3:5–6 says, "Trust in the LORD with all your heart and lean not on your own understanding; in all your ways submit to him, and he will make your paths straight" (NIV). Don't lean on human understanding, but on His ways. They are good and rightly aligned.

How does Paul remain confident through life's dark storms? Through a quiet trust in the only One who could carry him through it and bring him out alive.

What Is Confidence?

Merriam-Webster defines 'confidence' as, "a feeling or consciousness of one's powers or of reliance on one's circumstances. It is the quality or state of being certain." It is a firm trust. The word 'confidence' comes from the Latin word *confidentia*, meaning, "to put one's trust in someone."[54]

I have a childhood friend who is going through one of the darkest seasons of his life. After nineteen years of being with the same woman, ten years of marriage, and a daughter, what he thought would last forever suddenly came to a screeching halt. She decided to move out of the house, end the marriage, and start dating all over again. He is still madly in love with her. His text message to me last Saturday night was, "What a storm!"

There are times when even Christians are faced with life's dark storms. No one is exempt from the stormy night seasons of life when the path of life is almost not visible, and the clouds are so dark you can't see. If you are at that point in your life or have ever been there, you can relate to Paul in Acts 27.

The Holy Spirit gave Paul confidence in a dark season of raging storms in Acts 27. The opening verses reads like a logbook about ancient ships and seaman. Paul was a prisoner being transported to Rome to stand trial before Caesar for preaching the gospel. In Acts 27:4–7, the first signs of a storm rising appear. Paul warned the other prisoners of danger ahead: "Men, I can see that our voyage is going to be disastrous and bring great loss to ship and cargo, and to our own lives also" (Acts 27:10 NIV). It was after the Day of Atonement in the autumn—the time of year when sailing was dangerous. But the centurion ignored Paul's warning and continued to sail.

As Paul warned, the perfect storm arose and a "wind of hurricane force, called the Northeaster, swept down from the island" (Acts 27:14 NIV). It was dark for fourteen days and everyone on the ship lost hope except Paul. Paul assured them they would all survive the storm based on a vision he had received from the Lord (Acts 27:23).

As they approached land they dropped four anchors into the sea and prayed for daylight. Some of the sailors tried to jump ship pretending as though they were laying down anchors when they were really trying to save their lives. Paul recognized their plan and said to the centurion, "Except these abide in the ship, ye cannot be saved" (Acts 27:31 KJV). The soldier's cut the line and the boat drifted off. Paul urged them to eat after fourteen days of no food.

At daybreak, they spotted unfamiliar land and decided to try and run the ship ashore. The ship hit a reef and broke into pieces. The soldiers decided to kill the prisoners to prevent them from escaping (Acts 27:42), but the centurion who was "willing to save Paul kept them from their purpose" (Acts 27:43 KJV). He gave orders for everyone to swim for their lives and to grab pieces of the ship as floatation devices. Everyone made it to shore safely.

God Is the Only Anchor

Paul knew that during this dark storm God was with him. He had exhorted the prisoners to "be of good cheer" (Acts 27:22 KJV) for an angel of the Lord had told him none would die (Acts 27:23). The angel represented the presence of God, who promises in Scripture that He "is our refuge and strength, a very present help in trouble" (Psalm 46:1 KJV).

God involves Himself in the everyday affairs of people's life and is able to uphold His creation. God sees the end at the beginning (Isaiah 46:10). In other words, anything and everything people experience in life is a part of God's plan. Though the process may not be fun, God's plan must be respected.

Paul knew that whatever transpired during the storm would not prevent God's will or His Word from coming to fruition in his life.

Acts 27:29 ends by saying the sailors "wished for day" in the King James Version. 'Wished' is the Greek word *euchomai*, which means "to pray."[55] When in a night season in a raging storm, pray to the "anchor" of your soul. The writer of Hebrews affirms this concept: "We have this hope as an anchor for the soul, firm and secure" (Hebrews 6:19 NIV). Hope in Christ is the believer's security.

Prayer is also essential to every believer. The prophet Isaiah declared, "In repentance and rest is your salvation, in quietness and trust is your strength" (Isaiah 30:15 NIV).

Quietly trust God, your confidence. He is your anchor. He will bring you out of the storm and lead you to the destination He has ordained for you.

CHAPTER TWENTY-EIGHT

A Consistent Conclusion

Acts 28

God rarely allows people to see beyond the next step of faith. Sometimes, a person's present predicament does not look like His future promises. Inconsistent conditions cause people to doubt. However, the Holy Spirit is consistent, even when conditions are not.

I read a story about a lady named Myrtie Howell who was a faithful Christian from a poor family. She married at age seventeen, but her husband was killed in an accident. After her husband's death, she lost her home and had to work to support herself and her three kids. In her latter years, she ended up in a nursing home. A short time after that, her youngest son died. She became severely depressed and prayed to God to take her home. She had been faithful to God, but it just didn't seem that life had unfolded as she expected.

God heard her prayer and told her, "I'm not through with you yet! Write to prisoners." She began writing to prisoners and sharing Jesus Christ with them. Prison Fellowship gave her some more names, and she began corresponding with up to forty inmates a day. She became a one-woman ministry reaching into prisons all over America. She thought her life was over but God still had a plan.[56]

Myrtie Howell is an example of what it means to be consistent in faithfulness to God even when life's conditions are not favorable. She became a powerful missionary for God from her one-room apartment.

Dear friends, God never called Christian to be successful, but He has called them be consistent in faithfulness, to remain the same in one's pattern of behavior. This is the last chapter of Acts and Paul has remained consistent in his faithfulness to God.

The Conditions and the Incident

All of those who were on the ship made it to dry land. However, they were among strangers. It was cold, raining, and they are all wet but the natives were hospitable. The barbarians (anyone who was not considered Greek) received Paul and his wet companions warmly. The natives made a fire to provide warmth. In Acts 28:3–7, as Paul assisted the natives in building a fire, a snake slithered up from beneath the wood pile and bit Paul. The natives first accused Paul of being a murderer expecting him to die from the snakebite—but when he lived, they called him a god.

The Healing and the Arrival

Publius took Paul and his companions to his estate. He gave them lodging and food for three days. During the stay, Paul discovered that Publius's father was sick with a fever and dysentery (inflammation of the intestines that leads to severe diarrhea). Paul prayed first and then placed his hands on Publius's father—and healed him.

> *And it came to pass, that the father of Publius lay sick of a fever and of a bloody flux: to whom Paul entered in, and prayed, and laid his hands on him, and <u>healed</u> him.* — ***Acts 28:8 (KJV)***

Paul walked in apostolic authority, trusting the Holy Spirit would enable him to heal the man. He was carrying out a mandate in Acts 28 recorded by Jesus in Mark 16:17–18:

> *And these signs shall follow them that believe; In my name shall they cast out devils; they shall speak with new tongues; They shall take up serpents; and if they drink any deadly thing, it shall not hurt them; they shall lay hands on the sick, and they shall recover.* ***(KJV)***

Healing was immediate. However, healing for others occurs over time. There are two different words for healing in this section. Notice the word 'healed' in the next verse in Acts 28:

So when this was done, others also, which had diseases in the island, came, and were <u>healed</u>. — Acts 28:9 (KJV)

In Acts 28:8, the word for 'healed' is the Greek word *iaomai*, which means "to cure, heal or make whole."[57] The word for 'healed' in Acts 28:9, however, is a little different. It is the word *therapeuō*, which means "to serve, do service, or restore to health."[58]

The first word indicates the man in Acts 28:8 was healed immediately while the second hints at healing over a period of time.

The natives honored the shipwrecked mariners in many ways during their three-day stay and sent them away with supplies for their journey. In Acts 28:11, the men set out to travel on a ship of Alexandria whose sign was Castor and Pollux. They are known in Greek Mythology as the twin sons of Zeus and were considered gods of the sailors. They remained in Syracuse for three days and made additional stops (Acts 28:12).

They met brethren (Christian friends) and stayed with them seven days and then sailed with them toward Rome (Acts 28:14). On the outskirts of Rome, there were some Christians that heard of their arrival. Some came from as far as forty miles away to see Paul. When Paul entered the city of Rome, he was allowed to live wherever he wanted to and was assigned a guard. Paul accomplished a journey that he set out on many years prior. God promised Paul twice that he would make it to Rome and now God had delivered on His promise.

This scene was the fulfillment of a promise but not at all like Paul had imagined. He imagined he would enter the city a free man and openly preach to the masses. What God had planned was his visit to Rome under house arrest, with limited access to the people.

The Model of Ministry

In the remaining verses, Paul did what he had done throughout this complete study; he remained consistent with his witness of Jesus Christ. He met with Jewish leadership and defended his whole incarceration experience. He called them that they may understand. They told Paul that they never received letters stating anything bad about him, but they were interested in what he had to say.

The only thing they heard was that Christianity was a bad sect of Judaism. They agreed to meet with Paul again so he could explain the gospel to them. On the day of the meeting, the Jewish leaders brought their friends to Paul's house to hear what he had to say. Paul taught them all day, pointing out what Moses and the prophets had to say about Jesus Christ.

Some believed Paul and some refused to believe a word of it. When the unbelievers started arguing with each other, Paul said:

The Holy Spirit spoke the truth to your ancestors when he said through Isaiah the prophet: "Go to this people and say, 'You will be ever hearing but never understanding; you will be ever seeing but never perceiving. For this people's heart has become calloused; they hardly hear with their ears, and they have closed their eyes. Otherwise they might see with their eyes, hear with their ears, understand with their hearts and turn, and I would heal them.' Therefore I want you to know that God's salvation has been sent to the Gentiles, and they will listen!" (Acts 28:26–28 NIV).

Paul did what he was supposed to do. He may not have been successful, but he was faithful. He turned to the gentiles in Rome and began to share gospel with those that would receive it with open arms. Paul lived for two years in his rented house and welcomed everyone who came to visit (Acts 28:30). He consistently presented all matters of the Kingdom of God and taught about the Lord Jesus Christ (Acts 28:31).

Be Thankful and Take Courage in Crisis

One of the hardest things to do is to be appreciative and courageous in crisis. We want to quit because we "just don't feel like it." Paul remains consistently appreciative and courageous. (Philippians 4:12-13). Remember that God never calls us to be successful, but He does call us to be faithful (Revelations 2:10).

CONCLUSION

In the Center of His Will—and Unstoppable

There are times when our condition in life will not match our expected conclusion. God may not choose to work out His plans for us the way we think He should. However, as Christians we cannot always trust what we see. "For we walk by faith, not by sight" (2 Corinthians 5:7 KJV).

If anyone could have been disappointed with life, Paul was a good candidate. God promised him he would get to Rome to preach the gospel, and He made good on His promise but Paul did not anticipate the obstacles that would accompany the promise. God made good on His promise because Paul was consistent. God's promises are conditional. They are attached with the addendum that we would be found faithful. Paul teaches us to remain consistent and never quit what God has called us to do. God's calling for our lives is to be faithful not successful.

When we understand the will of God for our lives, we are held accountable to God for our actions. When we know His will and live our lives according to His will, we understand that God's ways are higher than our ways. We may not understand God's will, but we must consistently strive to be in the center of it (Isaiah 55:9, Jeremiah 29:11).

When we're in the center of God's will, we most fully experience the power of the Holy Spirit in our lives. The church in the first century AD was full of the power of the Spirit, and the result was a church movement that was unstoppable. However, the church today lacks power because she has abandoned the power given to her to become victorious. Believers must commit to turning back what has become a "museum for saints" to a living, breathing movement of followers of Jesus operating in the power of the Holy Spirit. This is the church God intended, and this kind of committed, sold-out, go-down-with-the-ship people of God is what will make a difference in other's lives.

The question for every Christian should be: Are you committed to this kind of movement of God? Don't waste another minute.

REFERENCES

Notes

1. Moltmann, Jorden, *Religion, Revolution, and the Future,* Scribners, 1969.

2. Barclay, William. "The Daily Study Bible Series Revised Edition—Acts of the Apostles." *DannyChestnut.* http://www.dannychesnut.com/Bible/Barclay/TH E%20ACTS%20OF%20THE%20APOSTLES.ht m

3. "3144. martys." *Blue Letter Bible.* https://www.blueletterbible.org/lang/lexicon/lexi con.cfm?t=kjv&strongs=g3144

4. "About Dr. King." *The King Center.* http://www.thekingcenter.org/about-dr-king

5. Clinton, Bobby. In "Five Characteristics of Movements" by Ryan Shaw. *Abandoned Times.* http://svm2.net/abandonedtimes/the-five-characteristics-of-movements/

6. "African Tradition, Proverbs, and Sanfoka." *The Spirituals Project*. University of Denver, 2004. In *Internet Archive*. https://web.archive.org/web/20110420131901/http://ctl.du.edu/spirituals/literature/sankofa.cfm

7. Turner, Steve. *The Band That Played On: The Extraordinary Story of the 8 Musicians Who Went down with the Titanic*. Nashville, TN, Thomas Nelson, 2011.

8. Bounds, E. M. *Power Through Prayer*. Merchant Books, 2013.

9. "4005. pentēkostē." *Blue Letter Bible*. https://www.blueletterbible.org/lang/lexicon/lexicon.cfm?t=kjv&strongs=g4005

10. "4342. proskartereō." *Blue Letter Bible*. https://www.blueletterbible.org/lang/lexicon/lexicon.cfm?t=nasb&strongs=g4342

11. "2842. koinonia." *Blue Letter Bible*. https://www.blueletterbible.org/lang/lexicon/lexicon.cfm?t=kjv&strongs=g2842

12. Barnes, Albert. "Barnes Notes Acts 2." *Bible Hub*. http://biblehub.com/commentaries/barnes/acts/2.htm from *Notes on the Bible by Albert Barnes* [1834]. Text Courtesy of Internet Sacred Texts Archive.

13. Bowman, Karlyn, and Jennifer Marsico. *"As the Tea Party Turns Five, It Looks a Lot Like the*

Conservative Base." 24 February 2014. *Forbes.* http://www.forbes.com/sites/realspin/2014/02/24/as-the-tea-party-turns-five-it-looks-a-lot-like-the-conservative-base/#636574865f72

14. Hayes, Charles. "Heaven is My Goal." *The Lyric Archive.* http://www.thelyricarchive.com/song/1008088-134312/Heaven-Is-My-Goal

15. Anonymous. "I Have Decided to Follow Jesus." *Hymnary.* http://www.hymnary.org/text/i_have_decided_to_follow_jesus

16. "4137. plēroō." *Blue Letter Bible.* https://www.blueletterbible.org/lang/lexicon/lexicon.cfm?t=kjv&strongs=g4137

17. "Polysyndeton." *Literary Devices.* http://literarydevices.net/polysyndeton/

18. Phillips, John. *Exploring Acts.* Moody Press, 1986, p.78–79.

19. "3170. megalynō." *Blue Letter Bible.* https://www.blueletterbible.org/lang/lexicon/lexicon.cfm?Strongs=G3170&t=KJV

20. "1249. diakonos." *Blue Letter Bible.* https://www.blueletterbible.org/lang/lexicon/lexicon.cfm?Strongs=G3170&t=KJV

21. "4134. plērēs." *Blue Letter Bible.* https://www.blueletterbible.org/lang/lexicon/lexicon.cfm?t=nasb&strongs=g4134

22. Clarke, Adam, and Ralph Earle. *Adam Clarke's Commentary on the Bible*. Grand Rapids, Baker Book House, 1967.

23. Jacobs, Joseph, and Ludwig Blau. "Holy Spirit." *Jewish Encyclopedia*. http://www.jewishencyclopedia.com/articles/783 3-holy-spirit

24. Smallwood, Richard. "Total Praise." In "Total Praise Lyrics." *MetroLyrics*. CBS Interactive. http://www.metrolyrics.com/total-praise-lyrics-richard-smallwood.html

25. "0496. antipiptō." *From NAS Exhaustive Concordance of the Bible with Hebrew-Aramaic and Greek Dictionaries,* The Lockman Foundation, 1998. *Lexicon Concordance*. http://lexiconcordance.com/greek/0496.html

26. Farley, Harry. "The Surprising Surge of Christianity in the Middle East." 11 January 2016. *Christianity Today*. http://www.christiantoday.com/article/the.surprising.surge.of.christianity.in.the.middle.east/76239.htm

27. Clarke, Adam. *The New Testament, of Our Lord and Saviour Jesus Christ* (vol. 1–3). Butterworth, 1817.

28. "Sanctification." *Bible Study Tools*. http://www.biblestudytools.com/dictionaries/bakers-evangelical-dictionary/sanctification.html

29. "3618. oikodomeō." *Blue Letter Bible.* https://www.blueletterbible.org/lang/lexicon/lexicon.cfm?t=kjv&strongs=g3618

30. "4151. pneuma." From *NAS Exhaustive Concordance of the Bible with Hebrew-Aramaic and Greek Dictionaries*, The Lockman Foundation, 1998. *Bible Hub.* http://biblehub.com/greek/4151.htm

31. Kuyper, Abraham. *The Work of the Holy Spirit*, William B. Eerdman's, 1941.

32. Scott, Jerry. "Faith That Guides Lessons from Moses." 29 April 2002. *Sermon Central* http://www.sermoncentral.com/sermons/faith-that-guides-lessons-from-moses-jerry-scott-sermon-on-faith-46063

33. Clark, Caesar. "Past Masters: Caesar A.W. Clark-Small Stature, Giant Message." 1 January 2016. *Preaching.* http://www.preaching.com/resources/articles/past-masters-caesar-a-w-clark-small-stature-giant-message/

34. MacArthur, John F. *Acts 1–28 MacArthur New Testament Commentary Two Volume Set.* Moody, 1996.

35. "873. aphoriz." *Blue Letter Bible.* https://www.blueletterbible.org/lang/lexicon/lexicon.cfm?t=kjv&strongs=g873

36. "37. hagiazō." *Blue Letter Bible.* https://www.blueletterbible.org/lang/lexicon/lexicon.cfm?t=kjv&strongs=g37

37. "3875. paraklētos." *Blue Letter Bible.* https://www.blueletterbible.org/lang/lexicon/lexicon.cfm?t=kjv&strongs=g3875

38. Wellman, Jack. "Bible Definition of Sin: How Does the Bible Define Sin or Sinning?" 14 June 2014. *Patheos.* http://www.patheos.com/blogs/christiancrier/2014/06/24/bible-definition-of-sin-how-does-the-bible-define-sin-or-sinning/

39. "2430. Ikonion." *Blue Letter Bible.* https://www.blueletterbible.org/lang/lexicon/lexicon.cfm?Strongs=G2430&t=KJV

40. "2559. kakoō." *Blue Letter Bible.* https://www.blueletterbible.org/lang/lexicon/lexicon.cfm?Strongs=G2559&t=KJV

41. "1485. ethos." *Blue Letter Bible.* https://www.blueletterbible.org/lang/lexicon/lexicon.cfm?Strongs=G1485&t=KJV

42. "2218. zygos." *Blue Letter Bible.* https://www.blueletterbible.org/lang/lexicon/lexicon.cfm?Strongs=G2218&t=KJV

43. Rich, Tracy R. "Halakhah: Jewish Law." *JewFaq.* http://www.jewfaq.org/halakhah.htm

44. "3948. paroxysmos." *Blue Letter Bible.* https://www.blueletterbible.org/lang/lexicon/lexicon.cfm?Strongs=G3948&t=KJV

45. "Navigate" *Merriam-Webster.* https://www.merriam-webster.com/dictionary/navigate

46. Brady, John. "What Are the Main Differences between Epicureanism and Stoicism?" 20 October 2015. *Quora.* https://www.quora.com/What-are-the-main-differences-between-epicureanism-and-stoicism

47. *Ibid.*

48. "Acts 17 Commentary." *Precept Austin.* http://www.preceptaustin.org/acts_17_commentary

49. "1097. ginosko." *Blue Letter Bible.* https://www.blueletterbible.org/lang/lexicon/lexicon.cfm?Strongs=G1097&t=KJV

50. "Acts 19:15." *Bible Hub.* http://biblehub.com/commentaries/acts/19-15.htm

51. "331. anathema." *Blue Letter Bible.* https://www.blueletterbible.org/lang/lexicon/lexicon.cfm?Strongs=G331&t=KJV

52. "Patience." *Oxford Dictionaries.* https://en.oxforddictionaries.com/definition/patience

53. "Consistent." *Merriam-Webster.* https://www.merriam-webster.com/dictionary/consistent?utm_campaign=sd&utm_medium=serp&utm_source=jsonld

54. "Confidence." *Merriam-Webster.* https://www.merriam-webster.com/dictionary/confidence

55. "2172. euchomai." *Blue Letter Bible.* https://www.blueletterbible.org/lang/lexicon/lexicon.cfm?Strongs=G2172&t=NLT

56. Perry, John. *God Behind Bars: The Amazing Story of Prison Fellowship.* Thomas Nelson, 2006.

57. "2323. iaomai." *Blue Letter Bible.* https://www.blueletterbible.org/lang/lexicon/lexicon.cfm?Strongs=G2323&t=KJV

58. "2390. therapeuō." *Blue Letter Bible.* https://www.blueletterbible.org/lang/lexicon/lexicon.cfm?Strongs=G2390&t=KJV

About the Author

The Reverend Dr. Oscar Terrance Moses is the second
child of the late Oscar Moses and Rosetta Moses-Hill
and the fifth generation to preach the gospel. He serves
as the 17th Pastor of the Mt. Hermon Missionary Baptist
Church, where his grandfather, the late Reverend Joseph
A. Allen, served as pastor for 41 years.

Dr. Moses is a graduate of Mendel Catholic Preparatory
High School of Chicago. He earned his Bachelor of
Science Degree in Criminal Justice with a minor in
Religious Studies from Southern Illinois University in
Carbondale. On June 6, 2000, he received his Master of
Arts in Theological Studies from McCormick
Theological Seminary. On May 21, 2001, he received a
Certificate of Completion for one extended unit of level
one CPE by the Association for Clinical Pastoral
Education, Inc. at Advocate South Suburban Hospital.
Dr. Moses is a Mckissick Carter Fellow graduate of the
United Theological Seminary, where he earned his
Doctor of Ministry Degree in 2014. His dissertation was
focused on *Preaching That Challenges Congregations to
Transform Community Hopelessness to Hope and
Beyond.*

Dr. Moses married his helpmeet, Jacqueline Marie, on
July 27, 1996. She has earned a master's degree in
Special Education from Saint Xavier University in
Chicago as well as a doctoral degree in Educational
Psychology from National Lewis University in Skokie,
Illinois.

Dr. Moses has a passion for soul-winning. His
commitment to teaching the Word of God has inspired

the development of W.A.R. (Word of God Applied
Rightly) Bible Study.

Dr. Moses is the President and CEO of Exodus
Unlimited. The mission of Exodus Unlimited is to
glorify our Lord and Savior, Jesus Christ, through
community empowerment. On January 17, 2007, the
University of Chicago Hospital recognized Exodus
Unlimited during the Dr. Martin Luther King Jr. Awards
Ceremony for providing After School Care to youth
within the Auburn Gresham Community. The After
School Care Program was created to reduce educational
apathy, gang activity, and low reading scores within the
community.

Dr. Moses serves as Moderator for the Christian Unity
Baptist District Association. He is the Chairman of
Evangelism for the Illinois National Baptist State
Convention and the former Coordinator for the
Evangelical Board Tent Revival for the National Baptist
Convention of America, Inc. Dr. Moses is currently an
adjunct professor at Trinity Christian College in Palos,
Illinois, teaching "Christian Worldview." Dr. Moses is a
member of Omega Psi Phi Inc. Fraternity.

Dr. Moses is a Bible-believing, God-trusting, and God-
fearing servant of the Lord. His favorite scripture is:
"Trust in the Lord with all thine heart; and lean not unto
thine own understanding. In all thy ways acknowledge
him, and he shall direct thy paths" (Proverbs 3:5-6 KJV).
It is evident that God is truly directing his path as he
continues to serve Him in spirit and in truth.

About Sermon To Book

SermonToBook.com began with a simple belief: that sermons should be touching lives, *not* collecting dust. That's why we turn sermons into high-quality books that are accessible to people all over the globe.

Turning your sermon series into a book exposes more people to God's Word, better equips you for counseling, accelerates future sermon prep, adds credibility to your ministry, and even helps make ends meet during tight times.

John 21:25 tells us that the world itself couldn't contain the books that would be written about the work of Jesus Christ. Our mission is to try anyway. Because, in heaven, there will no longer be a need for sermons or books. Our time is now.

If God so leads you, we'd love to work with you on your sermon or sermon series.

Visit www.sermontobook.com to learn more.

www.ingramcontent.com/pod-product-compliance
Lightning Source LLC
LaVergne TN
LVHW052017080426
835513LV00018B/2069